SHATTERED THEN SOARED

CORRINA R. LYNCH

DEDICATION

For my mother, Rosa Lee, whose love shaped my first breath and still guides me in your absence. Your spirit is my foundation.

For my father, Robert Lee, whose presence and lessons live on in me, even beyond this life. You are part of my beginning and remain part of who I am becoming

For my sister, Robin, whose strength and laughter still echo in my heart. You taught me resilience wrapped in tenderness.

For my niece, Janeexa, a bright light has gone too soon. Your memory reminds me

to hold life gently and love fiercely.

For my son, Ernest, and my daughter, Bilae— my heart in human form, my reason, my forever.

ACKNOWLEDGEMENTS

This book was not written in isolation. It was shaped by love, loss, survival, and the people who stood beside me—sometimes quietly, sometimes fiercely—while I found the courage to tell my truth.

I acknowledge my family, whose stories are woven through these pages. Our shared history, both beautiful and painful, gave this book its heartbeat. Thank you for the lessons, even the hard ones, and for the love that existed even when it didn't know how to show itself.

To my children, Ernest and Bilae—thank you for being my reason to heal, to grow, and to keep going. Your presence grounded me when the past felt heavy, and your love reminds me every day why breaking cycles matter.

To those who have walked with me through grief, family addiction, recovery, and becoming—thank you for holding space when words failed and for offering compassion instead of judgment. Your support mattered more than you know.

To every woman who has had to build strength where protection should have been—this book is for you. May you see yourself in these pages and know that your survival is not accidental. It is powerful.

And finally, I acknowledge myself—for telling the truth, for choosing healing over silence, and for having the courage to write what was once too painful to say aloud.

PROLOGUE

I've been broken in more ways than I can count. By men who said they loved me.

By friends who smiled in my face and whispered behind my back.

By a family who shared my blood but not my loyalty. I've buried my mother. I've watched

My daughter delivered a baby who never took a breath. I've cried in silence while pretending to be strong. I've been bruised, betrayed, and left to rebuild from rubble more than once. But I've also raised children who shine.

I've built a business from scratch. I've served my country with pride as a federal worker. I've survived what was meant to destroy me—and I did it with grace, grit, and God. This book is not about revenge.

It's about release. It's about the woman I became through every heartbreak, every loss, every lie. If you've ever been hurt, silenced, or underestimated—this is for you. Because healing isn't pretty. But it's powerful. And this is how I found mine.

CONTENTS

CHAPTER 1

MY PARENTS: SPOILED, LOVED & PROTECTED

I grew up knowing two things for certain:
my family loved me, and my family was dangerous.

My story begins in a home alive with warmth, laughter, and love.
Yes—chaos, loss, trauma, and survival came later.
But before life hardened me, it softened me.
Before I learned fear, I learned belonging.
Before I learned silence, I learned joy.

I was born in Newark, New Jersey, and raised in Baltimore, Maryland,
but neither place ever felt like my true home.
Home was the crowded house where loyalty meant survival and silence
protected every secret.
A house full of love and noise, affection and tension—where
everything existed at once and nothing was ever simple.

I was the unexpected one—the surprise baby who arrived after my
mother believed that chapter of her life had closed.
But life had other plans.

My mother was a Durham, North Carolina girl—light-brown skin, soft
hips, gentle by nature, deeply grounded.
She came from a **big family**, the kind where everybody knows
everybody's business, where love is loud, and opinions are louder.
Her people loved to gossip, assume, and stir the pot—but you had to
love them.
That was their way of staying connected, even when it was messy.

My father was from Suffolk, Virginia—chocolate-skinned,
curly-headed, and full of fire.

He grew up in a **smaller, funny-acting family** who didn't play about
boundaries.
His side would cut you off in a second—no warning, no explanation.

And honestly?
That's kind of how I am.

My father was **Blackfoot (Native American)**, and that part of him
showed up in his pride, his independence, and his refusal to be owned
by anyone.
His mother came from money—real money.
But my father never looked for anything from my grandmother.
He didn't want handouts.
He didn't want favors.
He didn't want to be taken care of.
He wanted to earn his own.
That was his code.
That was his backbone.

They were opposites in every way that mattered.
Her softness balanced his edge.
His strength shielded her gentleness.
And somehow, I was a blend of them both.

I have my mother's eyes and her hips,
and my father's looks, his attitude, and his curly hair.
Her softness lives in my gaze.
His fire lives in my presence.

I was the baby of eleven children—spoiled, protected, adored.
I never got beaten.
Never faced the punishments my siblings endured.
I was quiet, observant, careful—always trying to stay out of the storms
that moved through our home.
Mommy did everything for me.
Looking back, I was a princess.

And Daddy?
He treated me like royalty.
He carried my bags.
He opened doors.
He made sure I ate first.
If I cried, he stopped everything.

If I wanted something, he found a way to get it.
If I walked into a room, his whole face softened.

But that softness wasn't given to everyone.

My siblings got a different version of him.
He was harder on them—especially the boys.
He expected perfection.
He demanded respect.
He yelled.
He disciplined.
He pushed them in ways he never pushed me.

They got the fire.
I got the warmth.
They got the rules.
I got the exceptions.
They got the man shaped by survival.
I got the man softened by fatherhood.

I didn't understand it then.
I just knew I was loved differently protected differently.
But as I got older, I realized that the same man who made me feel untouchable
also made some of my siblings feel small, afraid, or unseen.

And that truth is complicated.

Behind the protection lived things no child should have to witness.
Some of my siblings struggled with addiction, battling demons I didn't yet have words for.
My father fought alcoholism, carrying pain that leaked into our lives in ways I could feel but not fully understand.
The house held love, but it also held darkness—secrets buried so deeply they became part of the walls.

And the truth is, **I didn't see much because I was young.**
Things happened before my time—things whispered about, denied, or buried under silence.

I grew up in the aftermath of storms I never saw, only the quiet that followed them.

There were things that happened behind closed doors.
Things that happened before I was born.
Things people avoided, softened, or refused to name.
I can only speak to what I experienced, the truth of growing up surrounded by loyalty, fear, love, and silence.

I was eleven years old when my father died.
A heart attack.
And I witnessed it.

I can still see it:
his eyes rolling back,
his body going still,
the room filling with panic and disbelief.
Paramedics pressing into his chest, performing CPR as if effort alone could keep him here.
I watched the man who made the world feel safe leave it right in front of me.

Losing him shattered me.
I didn't just lose my dad—I lost the only sense of safety I had ever known.
The house didn't just lose a man; it lost its anchor.
Laughter softened.
Protection shifted.
The world immediately felt colder.
Bigger.
More dangerous.

Childhood ended the moment I realized he wasn't coming back.

After he died, I learned things.

I never saw my father hit my mother.
I never witnessed physical violence.
What I saw was discipline—raised voices, a man who demanded respect.

Only later did the fuller truth emerge.
Through whispers.
Through siblings.
Through fragments of conversations spoken carefully—or not at all.

My father was abusive to my mother, continuously.
He drank heavily, while my mother never even smoked a cigarette.
He was abusive to some of my brothers, too—physically and
emotionally—leaving scars I didn't see until I was older.

That truth complicated my grief.
It forced me to hold two realities at once:
the man who made me feel protected,
and the man who caused pain I never saw.

I didn't grow up knowing that version of him.
But I grew into the truth of it.

Still, in my eyes, he was my hero.
And losing him at eleven was the first heartbreak I ever knew.

Life didn't fall apart all at once, it slowly cracked.
I didn't know then how much the love of those early years would
matter.
How it would become the standard I searched for.
The safety I would miss.
The absence I would spend years trying to understand.

Because when my father died, my childhood ended.
And soon... everything would change.

CHAPTER 2
SISTERS, LOVE, LOSS, DISTANCE & BECOMING

Sisterhood Is Complicated

Sisterhood is complicated.
It is love and distance.
Laughter and heartbreak.
Connection wrapped in misunderstanding.
Loyalty layered with wounds.

My sisters and I were shaped by the same mother, carved from the same history, marked by the same storms—yet life sent us into different battles, different choices, different ways of surviving.

I had three blood sisters—three women forever tied to me, three forces that helped shape the woman I became.
Each one taught me something different about love:
how it shows up,
how it disappears,
how it survives.

And I must say this with pride and truth:
my sisters were all smart.
Sharp in their own ways.
Wise in ways life didn't always honor,
but ways I always saw.

The Oldest — Love with Edges

My oldest sister was the general of the house—
the loudest voice, the strongest presence,
the one who demanded excellence and accepted nothing less.

Growing up with her felt like training—
boot camp disguised as sisterhood.

Her love wasn't soft.
But it was steady.
Structured.
Disciplined.
Relentless.

She taught me how to cook—real cooking.
Seasoning with intention.
Tasting as you go.
"Because a girl needs to know how to feed herself."

She taught me how to clean—
moving furniture, scrubbing corners,
washing walls until they shined.
"Don't half-do nothing," she'd say.
And I didn't.

She taught me how to wash clothes—
separating loads, treating stains,
folding with pride.

To her, these were chores.
To me, they were lessons in womanhood.

When I became a mother, she showed up for my children—
fed them, watched them, protected them in ways she couldn't always
protect me.
My children adore her.
Her love came through action, not affection.

Adulthood revealed a deeper truth:
sometimes she wasn't upset with me—
she was upset with our mother.
Old wounds.
Unspoken pain.
Unresolved childhood shadows.

And because I was the youngest—
the one she felt safest with—
I became the place her hurt landed.

The family would say,
"You know what she's been through."
"You have to understand her."

And I did understand her trauma.
But understanding someone's wounds
does not mean allowing them to wound you.

Two truths can exist at the same time:
she is hurting—
and she has hurt me.

I learned to set boundaries—
not out of anger,
but out of survival.

I love her.
But I love myself too.

From her, I learned discipline, strength,
and how to stand firm in my truth.

The Middle — The One I Lost Slowly

She died of fentanyl.
She hadn't always been on drugs.
She was the heartbeat of warmth.
Loving, funny, nurturing—the sister who fed people, mothered
everyone, and cared deeply even when her own soul was tired.
She moved through life with an easy light.

I always thought she was beautiful—
light skinned with dimples, a smile that arrived before her words.
The lightest of all the sisters, as if brightness had chosen her twice.

13

She had a running joke, her signature line:
"Can I borrow twenty dollars?"
And every time, it made us laugh—even when sometimes I said no,
not out of meanness, but because I didn't always know what she might
use it for.

We weren't as close as we once were—
not because of anything bad,
but because life carried me to another state,
and time stretched itself quietly between us.

She was our mother's favorite—
their birthdays only a day apart,
bonded in ways that felt unspoken but obvious.

But she carried a pain that no one ever healed.
She was the one on the phone when our father died—
the last voice he heard before the silence.
He said his chest hurt.
Then he hung up.
That moment never loosened its grip on her.

Her mind became a harder place to live.
What began as survival slowly blurred into escape.
She didn't want to die.
She just wanted the pain to stop.

And I watched her fade in pieces—
a little here, a little there—
until the girl I grew up with
became someone I could only reach in memories.

By the time the call came,
I had already been grieving for years.

I was on a women's church meeting—
surrounded by prayer, scripture, and sisterhood—
when my phone lit up with my brother's name.

I stepped away quietly,
thinking it was something small,
something ordinary.

But his voice was trembling, thin,
carrying a truth he didn't know how to hold.

"They found her."
A pause that felt like the world stopped breathing.
Then the words that shattered everything:
"She's gone."

I started crying so hard—
the kind of cry that comes from the deepest place,
the place where love and fear and helplessness live together.
My body folded under the weight of it.
I couldn't catch my breath.
I couldn't hear anything but my own grief.

And then came the part that broke me in a different way—
the coroner's office.
The coldness of it.
The formality.
The way they spoke like they were reading from a script.

They told us they couldn't identify her.
She didn't have ID on her.
My sister—
a whole human being,
a mother, a daughter, a sister, a soul—
reduced to "unidentified female."

As if her life didn't matter.
As if her story could be erased
because she didn't have a piece of plastic in her pocket.

It made me so upset—
angry, hurt, insulted on her behalf.

How could they not know her?
How could they not see her?
We knew her by her laugh,
by her dimples,
by the way she said our names.
But to them, she was a body without a name.

That part cut deep.
It felt like losing her twice—
first to the pain she carried,
and then to a system that couldn't recognize her humanity.

Two words changed everything.
But the way the world handled her afterward
left a bruise I still feel.

I lost more than a sister—
I lost the girl she used to be,
the laughter, the meals she cooked,
the way she loved children,
the way she loved us.

I lost the version of her who danced in kitchens,
who braided hair with gentle hands,
who believed she could outrun the hurt
if she just kept moving.

Her death broke us.
But her life blessed me forever.

I carry her warmth, her softness, her kindness
in the quietest parts of myself.
And sometimes, when I'm alone,
I hear her laugh—
that bright, familiar sound—
and for a moment,
she's here again,
light as ever,

borrowing twenty dollars,
reminding me that love doesn't disappear.
It just changes shape
and finds a new place to live inside you.

The Youngest — Still Here

She is the youngest of the three—
the fearless one, a warrior born swinging.
Disabled but brilliant.
Chaotic but unforgettable.
Sharp-tongued, yet fiercely loyal.

She was always the glamorous one,
with bright skin that caught the light before she ever spoke.
My mirror.
My reminder of everything addiction tried—
and failed—to steal.

People used to say we looked alike all the time.
Same face. Same expressions. Same spark.

Until drugs began to change her—
until that familiar light faded behind exhaustion and struggle.

Addiction reached for her, too.
I almost lost her.
Almost buried her.
Almost lived that nightmare twice.

I remember visiting her and carrying heartbreak in silence—
because even though she was still alive,
I couldn't have my sister the way I deserved.

Addiction built a wall between us,
and it hurt seeing someone so full of life trapped behind it.

We argued.
We clashed.

We loved hard.
We fought loudly.

I remember how she used to wear my clothes,
and how angry I would get.
If I could go back,
she could wear anything she wants—
no questions, no anger, just love.

She almost died.
And the fear of losing her after losing my other sister
nearly broke me.

But she fought.
And I fought with her.

She chose rehab.
She chose healing.
She chose life.

Now, when I see her, she always says,
"You're so beautiful, girl,"
and every time, it still brightens my day.

Today, she is doing the work—
reclaiming herself piece by piece.

From her,
I learned resilience in its rawest form.

What They Left in Me

Three sisters.
Three lessons.

One gave me strength—
taught me the power of boundaries.

One gave me grief—
showed me the quiet grace that loss demands.

One gave me survival—
handed me hope when the world felt empty.

I did not leave sisterhood untouched.
I carry its scars.
But I also carry its shaping.
Its awakening.
Its becoming.

And the truth that still sits in the softest part of me is this:
I wish I could have my sisters the way life is supposed to be.
Whole.
Healthy.
Here.
Laughing, arguing, loving, living—together.
The way little girls imagine adulthood will look
before life teaches them otherwise.

But even without that picture-perfect ending,
I carry them.
All three.
In my memory,
in my spirit,
in the woman I became because of them.

And somehow,
I am still here—
standing tall,
holding all of them inside me.

CHAPTER 3

BROTHERS: LOVE, DISTANCE & TRUTH

I was blessed with seven brothers, each admirable in his own way—
for reasons rooted in character, not perfection.
They carried our mother's fire in seven different ways.

Growing up, I thought being the baby sister meant having seven
protectors—seven shields, seven men who would guard my heart and
keep me safe.
I thought love meant coverage.
That someone would step in before I ever had to.
That being surrounded by men meant I would never stand alone.

But real life wasn't a movie.

And instead of being protected, I learned how to protect myself.

Because protection was something people said, not something I
consistently felt.
Having seven brothers didn't mean seven people stood up for me—it
meant seven people assumed someone else would.
Everyone thought I was covered, so no one checked.

I learned early that being surrounded by men didn't guarantee safety—
it guaranteed expectation.
Expectation that I'd be strong.
Expectation that I'd endure.
Expectation that I wouldn't need too much, say too much, or ask too
many questions.

Love in this house often came with conditions—hierarchy, silence,
control disguised as concern.

Some of my brothers spent time in prison.
That's part of our story too.

And when that's your reality, there are unspoken rules.
One thing you could never do was talk badly about my mother's boys.
She loved them fiercely, protectively, without hierarchy.
They were her sons before their mistakes, before consequences, before anyone else's opinion.

That love was powerful—but it created imbalance.
Accountability wasn't always even.
Truth was sometimes softened.
Silence became loyalty.

My mother was also jealous of the wives.
Not petty jealousy—emotional, territorial love.
The kind that comes from a woman who gave everything to her sons and didn't know how to loosen her grip when other women entered their lives.

That dynamic lived under everything:
conversations, alliances, what was defended, what was ignored.

I didn't understand it then.
I do now.

I was closest to the youngest.
We grew up side by side.
Same house.
Same chaos.
Same storms.

But closeness didn't equal consistency.
And laughter didn't equal protection.

That's when I learned the truth:

**I wasn't being raised to be protected—
I was being trained to survive.**

And I did.

THE YOUNGEST — MY YOUNGEST
BROTHER SAID WE ARE CLOSE

My youngest brother said we are close.
And in some ways, we are—by history.
Same air. Same chaos. Same upbringing.

But closeness does not equal consistency.
And love without consistency is just confusion pretending to be
connection.

His care runs hot and cold.
Warm when it's convenient.
Distant when accountability shows up.

He carries assumptions about me that aren't true and treats them like
facts.

What complicates it is that he sees my growth.
He encouraged my move.
He praises my work.
He names my wins.

And still—recognition does not equal consistency.

When the world turned against him, I stood firm.
I defended him.
I spoke his name with loyalty even when it cost me.
I saw his wounds even when he tried to hide them.
I understood his pain before he understood himself.

I'm the one he calls when something needs to get done.
When it's urgent.
When follow-through matters.
I show up.
I execute.
I handle the business.

Yes—he pays me.
And I appreciate that.
But money doesn't explain dependence.

Assumptions ruin relationships.
And he lets them speak louder than conversation.

I love him, but communication is not optional.
If there's an issue, we address it.
If not, I move accordingly.

Some of the tension between us makes more sense now.
My father was abusive to some of my brothers—
not all of them, not in the same ways,
but enough to shape how anger moved through our house.

Because I was the baby, because I was protected differently,
resentment grew in places I didn't understand.

He would mess with me—small things.
Like going to the donut shop and buying all strawberry donuts,
knowing good and well, I only eat glazed.

It sounds small. Almost funny.
But every time he did, he got in trouble.

And that mattered.

To him, I wasn't just his sister.
I was proof of uneven protection.

THE SECOND-TO-THE-BABY — LOVE, HATE & MEMORY

He's funny.
Naturally.
Humor has always been his shield.

But humor didn't erase the harm.

Our relationship lived on extremes—
love on one end,
violence on the other.

We loved hard.
And fought harder.

He was the one who kicked me.
Not the youngest.
Not the oldest.
The one caught in between—
old enough to know better,
young enough to act without thinking.

He kicked me,
and my father had a heart attack
trying to protect me.

At the time, I didn't understand how those two moments were
connected.
I was too young to know that one act could ripple that far.

But for him, that moment followed him.
It created confusion between him and my father—
love tangled with guilt,
protection tangled with regret.

When my father later died,
that moment came back heavier.
Not as anger—
as regret.

The kind that doesn't get resolved
because there's no one left
to resolve it with.

I don't have issues with him today.
But I don't rewrite history.

And his children—
they have always been mine.
Not like mine.
They are.

That bond never fractured when we did.
Adult conflict never crossed that line.
And it never will.

THE SAGITTARIUS BROTHER — WORK WITHOUT WARMTH

Another brother and I are both Sagittarius.
Normally, I get along with Sagittarians.
But with him, we just don't like each other.

No betrayal.
No explosion.
Just friction that never softened.

What we do share is work ethic—
the same drive to build and run something of our own.

He's liked the most, which means people defend him no matter what
he does.
He's also convinced my mom left us millions of dollars, and I'm hiding
it.

Completely delusional.
I don't argue with it.
I let it live where it belongs—
in imagination, not reality.

THE SECOND-TO-THE-OLDEST —
SUCCESS, COMPARISON & CLARITY

Another brother has always been successful—
in the movie industry, in life.

He's been a celebrity to the family
for as long as I can remember.

In our family, success wasn't just admired—
it was worshipped.

His success became currency.
A badge.
A shield.

My mother compared me to him often.
Not to hurt me—
but because success was treated like a measuring stick.

When someone becomes a celebrity in the family,
the rules bend around them.
Their mistakes soften.
Their words carry weight.

He once told me others didn't like me.
Then said he didn't either.

Later, he asked for forgiveness.
I laughed—
not from cruelty,
but clarity.

I don't absorb attacks quietly.
I don't internalize judgments
from people who never asked questions.

Still—
he shows up.

Support.
Gifts.
Consistency.

That matters.

And his daughter—
my niece—
is my best friend.
Her loyalty is steady.
Untouched by adult conflict.

His success is his.
My strength is mine.
They are not the same currency.

THE OLDEST — ADMIRATION, AUTHORITY & DISTANCE

My oldest brother once treated me like his daughter.
That was the role he chose.

He protected me.
Corrected me.
Watched me closely.

For a while, I felt covered.
Then protection became control.
Authority replaced care.

Here's the complicated truth:
I admire him while he judges me.

He's always been admired—
the financially successful one,
the "CEO," in my mother's words.

Yes, I'm spoiled.
And I've always made my own money.
Sometimes I feel entitled—
because my parents gave me everything they could.

All of that can be true at once.

And his daughter—
my niece—
has always been my best friend.

Children were never collateral.
Whatever distance exists between adults
stops with us.

DOING ME CHANGED EVERYTHING

Choosing myself didn't create distance.
It created clarity.

I didn't cut anyone off.
I just stopped shrinking.

I don't chase understanding.
I don't audition for acceptance.

I show up as myself—
unfiltered, grown, healed.

I love them.
And I'm still doing me.

My peace is not negotiable.
My boundaries are not optional.
My worth is not up for debate.

And the family adjusted.

I didn't demand respect.
I embodied it.

And everything around me
shifted to match.

THE TRUTH THAT HOLDS IT ALL TOGETHER

I love my brothers.
Every single one of them.

They are smart.
Disciplined.
Builders.
Men who commit.
Married for decades—legacies.

I will brag about my siblings
even when I can't stand some of them.

Pride doesn't require closeness.
Respect doesn't require agreement.

Distance no longer feels like rejection.
It feels like clarity.

I am my mother's sweetness
and my father's fire.

Still loving.
Still standing.
Still true.

CHAPTER 4

THE FIRST MAN WHO TAUGHT ME HOW LOVE COULD HURT

The first man who mistreated me—outside of my brothers—was my son's father.

We started dating in high school. I would call him my high school sweetheart, even though our relationship was complicated from the very beginning.

I was in the ninth grade.
He was in the twelfth.

He was popular, a varsity basketball player, and I think that made me want him more. My mother had always instilled in me the importance of being with someone accomplished—someone driven, like my brothers. In my young mind, he fit that image.

He was shy, but he never had trouble speaking about my body, my physique. At the time, I confused that attention with affection.

We stayed together for about seven years. It was a strange relationship—long-distance, inconsistent, always changing shape. I met his family early on: his brother and his mother. I loved his mother deeply. She became like a second mother to me. May she rest in heaven.

She believed I was good for him.
And she loved her grandson until the day she passed away.

After he graduated from high school, he went to college in Colorado to play basketball. We stayed connected through letters and collect calls. When he came home, we spent time together like nothing had changed.

Eventually, he transferred to a local college in our hometown. By then, I had already graduated and was attending hair school.

Not long after, he began playing for a school in Pennsylvania.

That was when I became pregnant with our son.

He was our blessing—though neither of us felt ready. He didn't want a child. He felt we were too young. And if I'm honest, I didn't want a child either—not at that time.

But by the time I realized how far along I was, abortion was no longer an option.

I told my mother. She looked at me calmly and said,
"It's not the end of the world."

He was away when our son was born. He asked that I name him after him. And I did. My son became his junior.

Things began to change.

He started receiving invitations to professional camps—Chicago, Washington. He went to all of them. I went with him to one camp and stood quietly on the sidelines of a world that was opening up for him and slowly closing to me.

I met men whose names carried weight. I smiled. I supported him. But inside, I already knew.

This was temporary.

Not the opportunity.
Not the dream.
Me.

I felt it in my body before I admitted it to myself. The way he no longer reached for me. The way his future didn't include space for us—only space for himself.

Eventually, he chose another woman over me.
Not suddenly.
Not cruelly.
But clearly.

Over time, I had to face a truth that hurt more than rejection itself.
The women he admired, the women he pursued, the women he desired
did not look like me.

I had to confront the reality that he didn't like Black women—
not in the way that builds a life, chooses commitment, or honors
partnership.

That realization shattered something inside me.

Because it wasn't about my beauty.
It wasn't about my loyalty.
It wasn't about what I offered.

I was beautiful.
I was loving.
I was devoted.
I had carried his child.

And still, I was not chosen

That kind of rejection doesn't scream.
It settles.

It teaches you to disappear quietly while still standing right there

We didn't stay together much longer after that. The ending wasn't
dramatic—it was inevitable. But even after we separated, I remained
close to his family.
They helped raise my son in real, tangible ways.
They babysat.
They showed up.
They supported me when I needed it.

His mother loved her grandson deeply, fully, without condition, until the day she passed away. She treated him like a gift, not a burden. And knowing my son was loved like that mattered more to me than words can explain.

I will also say this truthfully:
He was a good provider.

He took care of me financially for over sixteen years. He made sure our son was supported. He showed up in that way, even though he didn't want to pursue me as a partner.

For a long time, I wondered if that came from guilt.

But then my son told me something his father once said to him:
"I will always take care of your mom if I am able to do so."

And that mattered.

Because it told me his support wasn't just an obligation—it was respect. It was a responsibility. It was his way of honoring the role I played in his life, even if he couldn't love me the way I needed.

Loving him also taught me something I didn't realize I was learning at the time.

It taught me how to tolerate emotional absence.

I learned how to stay connected to someone who was only halfway present.

How to accept inconsistency as normal.

How to confuse distance with maturity.

I learned how to shrink my needs so they wouldn't feel like burdens. And that lesson followed me.

What was familiar became comfortable.
And what was comfortable became dangerous.

Because once you learn how to love without being fully loved back, you stop recognizing absence as absence.
You call it patience.
You call it loyalty.
But it was loneliness.

I don't know exactly when I moved on.
There was no clear moment.
No announcement.
No dramatic release.

I just know that when he tried to come back to me, the feelings I once carried were gone.

Not replaced by anger.
Not replaced by bitterness.
Just gone.

He once told me I was an amazing mother—and an amazing grandmother.
I said, "I know."

Not from ego, but from certainty.

Then I told him what needed to be said:
"You need to do better being part of this journey. Money is not the only thing a child needs."

Because provision without presence is incomplete.
Love requires participation.
Parenting is more than paying bills.

What hurt the most was this he always put his friends first.
Before me.
Before showing up fully.

Before choosing responsibility over convenience.

That was the part that truly upset me—not the end of the relationship, but the lack of priority.

Because when someone consistently chooses everyone else, what they're really saying is that you—and the family you created together—come last.

And I won't compete for space in a life I helped build.

Today, I'm not mad at him.
I don't carry resentment anymore.
I don't replay the rejection.
I don't ask why I wasn't chosen.

Some people are not meant to be.
Not because anyone failed.
Not because love wasn't real.
But because timing, capacity, and willingness didn't align.

What we shared brought my son into this world.
What we survived taught me powerful lessons.
And what we released allowed me to move forward.

And that is enough.

CHAPTER 5
WHEN STABILITY ISN'T SAFETY

I didn't jump from one relationship into the next.
It took two years before the next man entered my life.
Two years of working.
Mothering.
Surviving.

Two years of learning how to function without romance while still carrying the residue of the last love I hadn't fully unpacked.

I wasn't rushing.
I wasn't searching.
I wasn't lonely in the way people assume.
But I also wasn't healed.

After my son's father, my life didn't feel dramatic—it felt heavy. I was raising a child. I was building stability. There wasn't space for heartbreak to fall apart loudly, so it settled quietly inside me.

The basketball player represented movement—travel, distance, dreams bigger than the space I lived in.
But he also represented uncertainty.
Waiting.
Hoping.
Adjusting my expectations so I wouldn't feel disappointed.

Loving him taught me endurance. It taught me how to stay connected to someone who wasn't fully available and call it a strength.

So when that relationship finally ended, I told myself I wanted the opposite.

I didn't want unpredictability.
I didn't want waiting.

I didn't want to feel optional.
I wanted stability.

So when the next man appeared—calm, consistent, clear about wanting me—I felt relief.

He wasn't chasing dreams across states.
He wasn't emotionally distant.
He didn't make me guess where I stood.
He was present.

And after two years of standing on my own, that presence felt reassuring.

What I didn't realize was that I wasn't choosing love.
I was choosing relief.

Relief from uncertainty.
Relief from emotional absence.
Relief from carrying everything alone.

The basketball player taught me how to wait.
The next man promised I wouldn't have to.

And that promise mattered more to me than it should have.

Because I hadn't healed the part of me that believed love required endurance. I hadn't questioned why familiarity still felt safer than freedom.

So when closeness became constant, I called it devotion.
When concern became questioning, I called it care.
When attention became control, I called it commitment.

I didn't see the shift happening.
I was moving from emotional absence into emotional control.

And because both required me to shrink parts of myself, my body didn't immediately recognize the danger.

It felt familiar.

The basketball player took up space in the world and left little room for me.

The man who followed took up space in my world and slowly left little room for anything else.

One abandoned me emotionally.
The other consumed me emotionally.

But both taught me the same lesson—before I understood it:

I had learned how to make myself smaller for love.

I didn't walk into abuse because I was weak.
I walked into it because I was trying to protect myself from pain I didn't yet know how to heal.

And the man who followed wasn't a contrast to my past.
He was its continuation.

CHAPTER 6

HIS HANDS AND HIS WORDS

Love didn't arrive loudly; it came disguised as familiarity.
But sometimes, it breaks your foundation.

My first marriage didn't start in chaos.
Most storms don't begin with thunder.

He came into my life gentle, charming, and attentive.
Soft words.
Warm hands.
Promises that looked like safety.

But slowly, quietly, the warmth turned into warnings.
The promises turned into control.
The charm turned into shadows.

His anger reminded me of home.
His shouting echoed the walls I grew up in.
And the way I shrank around him felt like a muscle memory reaction
I learned from watching my mother shrink around my father.

At first, he didn't hit me.
It began with words.

Sharp, belittling, humiliating words.
Jokes that weren't jokes.
Comments meant to weaken me.
Accusations meant to scare me.
Verbal blows that bruised places fists couldn't reach.

I didn't know it then, but I had married my trauma.
I chose what felt familiar—not what felt safe.
And once verbal blows became normal, the physical ones followed.

But even then… I stayed.
Because I was raised to endure pain, not escape it.
Raised to hold a marriage together, even if it tore me apart.

But endurance is not strength.
Leaving is.

And the day I walked away, I didn't know it yet—but I had taken the first step toward saving my own life.

Before Him — The Woman I Was

Before I met him, I was 24, going on 25—beautiful inside and out, confident, radiant, vibrant.
My walk turned heads.
My beautiful physique—graceful curves, strength, and elegances spoke without words.
My energy lit rooms.
My spirit glowed.
My confidence came from the love poured into me during childhood.

I wasn't looking for validation.
I was looking for partnership.
Family.
Stability.
Love.

To be chosen felt like love.
So, when he chose me, I chose him.

How I Met Him And The Guilt That Followed

I met him through his cousin.
I had briefly dated the cousin, nothing serious.
But I regretted that decision for years.
I was young, and because the cousin was temporary, I didn't think it

was a problem.
I take full responsibility for that decision.

Still, I carried guilt, wondering if I had crossed an invisible line.
Sometimes I wondered if he used that guilt to punish me later.
I had unhealed wounds, especially my issues with my brothers.
These were not excuses, just the truth.
But nothing I did justified what he would become.

Connected at the Hip, My Son and I

Before he came along, I had my son.
My first love.
My protector.
My shadow.
We were inseparable.

And when my ex entered the picture, my son didn't like him from the start—not from jealousy, but instinct.
Children see what adults pretend not to.

As things worsened, my son's instinct turned into resentment—not toward me, but toward what he saw me tolerate.
He watched me stay too long.
He watched me leave and return.
He watched me shrink.
And it hurt him in ways I wouldn't understand until years later.

The Beginning of the End

He was charming when he wanted to be.
Chocolate skin.
Soft curls.
Shy eyes.
He looked safe.

I thought we balanced each other—my fire with his quiet, my
confidence with his insecurity.
But he didn't admire my confidence.
He feared it.
He hated my ambition.
He hated that men desired me.
He hated that I could survive without him.
He was even jealous of my male cousins.

Arguments came from nowhere.
Mood swings snapped like rubber bands.
Accusations rained like storms.

And still… I married him.

A Warning Dressed as a Promise

The first wedding was huge.
Twenty people stood in the wedding party,
and 120 guests filled the room.
It was catered,
tables dressed in linens and centerpieces,
champagne flowing, laughter rising.

It looked like joy.
It looked like triumph.
It looked like love.

My mother spent her hard earnings for her baby girl,
wanting me to shine,
wanting me to be cherished.
Her sacrifice was poured into flowers, dresses, food, and music.

His brother raised a glass in a toast:
"She is the woman for him."
The guests clapped,
the cameras flashed,
and the moment was sealed in memory.

But deep down inside,
we both wore regret on our faces.

After the vows, the music, the applause,
I sat in the limo and told my maid of honor I wasn't happy.
She tried to comfort me:
"You can always get money, you can't always get love."

Later, at the hotel,
we opened our gift financial blessings, envelopes of money,
boxes wrapped in ribbons.
It should have felt like abundance,
but instead it felt like weight.

Because he had lost his job,
the honeymoon my brother gifted us at a resort never happened.
Instead, we ended up at the casino.

The lights were blinding,
the machines loud,
the air thick with smoke and desperation.
It wasn't romance.
It wasn't joy.
It was survival disguised as entertainment.

At first, we tried to pretend it was fun—
laughing at the blinking machines,
ordering drinks,
acting like newlyweds.
But beneath the surface,
the tension was already boiling.

Soon, the money became the argument.
Every chip, every hand, every spin of the wheel
was another reminder of what we didn't have.
And in that moment,
we fought like cats and dogs.
Voices rose,
hands flying,
anger spilling out in front of strangers.

Security had to pull us apart.
The flashing lights and ringing bells
became the soundtrack to our chaos.
People stared,
whispered,
watched as our marriage unraveled in public
before it had even begun.

He knew I was afraid of him.
He knew the power he carried in my silence.
But I always stood up for myself.
And that defiance—
that refusal to shrink—
made him even more upset.

The casino became more than a place of chance.
It became a mirror.
A reflection of what our marriage would be:
loud, chaotic,
filled with smoke and shadows,
with security always needed to separate us
before the damage went too far.

That night,
I realized the honeymoon wasn't canceled.
It was replaced.
Replaced with fear,
with fighting,
with a warning I could no longer ignore.

The next morning,
I woke up surrounded by gifts and envelopes,
symbols of blessing and hope.
But the room felt heavy,
the silence louder than the casino noise.

The boxes stacked neatly in the corner
looked less like abundance
and more like reminders of what we had already lost.

Barely an hour after the wedding, he had said:
"You want to argue like a man? Then I'll treat you like one."
That was the moment love died,
and fear moved in.

Fight — The Pot Incident

A few months after the marriage, we were at his family's house. Too many people crowded the room, too many eyes watching, too much pressure pressing in. The argument came fast. Voices rose. Names were thrown like stones. The walls seemed to close around me. Then he hit me—because he loved showing off in front of his family. The shock froze in the air. Instinct took over. I defended myself by grabbing a pot from the stove and hitting him in the head. The clang echoed louder than the shouting. But no one moved. No one stopped it. Only his best friend stepped in. My sister was there— watching, silent. Later, they blamed me for what he did. He called me names, out loud, in front of everyone. As if humiliation could erase his violence. As if shame could make it mine.

I left the party alone. The night air felt unreal, like I had stepped out of my own body. My hands wouldn't stop shaking. No one followed. No one asked if I was okay. I sat in my car, the door closing like a seal against the noise inside the house. The silence was deafening, but it wasn't peaceful, it was emptiness. I could have died. I could have gone to jail. But I still stayed.

The Financial Cracks — His Instability

The cracks were never just in the bills. They were in the walls, in the ceilings, in the very foundation of our life together. Every overdue notice was another fracture. Every broken promise was another splinter in the beams. Every lost job was another hole in the roof. The house we lived in became a metaphor. From the outside, it looked whole—a family, a marriage, a home. But inside, it was crumbling. The paint couldn't hide the damage. The laughter couldn't drown out the leaks. The smiles couldn't cover the rot.

The floors sagged under the weight of his instability. The doors slammed with his moods. The windows rattled with every argument. The roof leaked with every betrayal. I patched and patched, stretching dollars like plaster, stretching patience like nails. But no matter how many times I repaired, the cracks kept spreading. The walls kept breaking. The roof kept leaking. The love kept drowning.

It was as if the house itself knew—love built on instability cannot stand. The beams bent under the strain. The foundation shifted with every lie. The rooms echoed with emptiness, even when we were inside them. And one day, I realized: I wasn't living in a home. I was living in ruins. A collapsing structure, a place where scarcity and cruelty were the wallpaper of my life. The financial cracks were emotional cracks. The house was the marriage. And both were falling apart, piece by piece, until nothing was left but rubble and the memory of what should have been.

Pregnancy, Loss, Betrayal & God's Mercy

His violence caused miscarriages.
Each loss was a silent wound,
a grief I carried in my body and in my soul.
I learned that trauma doesn't just bruise the skin—
it settles in the womb,
it steals futures before they can arrive.

Then I became pregnant with my daughter Daja—
my prayer baby.
I whispered hope into her tiny heartbeat,
believing she would be the redemption of all the pain.
But at five months, I went into labor.
Too early.
Too fragile.
She didn't survive.

I buried more than a child that day.
I buried the dream of safety,
the illusion that love could protect me.

While I grieved, he cheated openly.
He told another woman:
"That bitch can't even hold a baby."
The cruelty was sharper than any blade.

Before I even healed,
six weeks passed,
and he forced himself on me again.
I became pregnant again.

This time, my daughter was born at 1 pound 6 ounces—
tiny, fighting, fragile.
Her body was smaller than my hand,
her cry barely a whisper.
But God covered her.
She survived.
My miracle girl.

I thought her survival would soften him,
make him see the mercy we had been given.
But instead, it made him spiral—
more cheating,
more violence,
more lies.
The miracle that should have changed him
only revealed how broken he truly was.

I finally left.
Packed my children.
Moved in with my mom.
Escaped.

Three days later, he came to my job—
stood in the lobby, patients waiting, coworkers watching.
He yelled,
"Bitch, bring your ass here!"

I yelled back,
"Leave before I call the police."

He said,
"I don't give a damn."

Later, he followed me again—
cornered me in an elevator,
bent my finger backward,
threatened me until someone called the police.

He was arrested.
I resigned from that job immediately.

After that, I didn't want to keep involving my mom.
So I went back home.

That's when he locked me in the closet
and told me he loved me so much.
Love twisted into control.
Obsession disguised as devotion.

After the closet, he took my daughter.
He kidnapped her—
then dropped her off with a family member.

I cried until I couldn't breathe.
My chest felt like it was caving in,
my body shaking with sobs that had no sound left.

That's when I knew—
this wasn't love.
It was an obsession.
And it was dangerous.

Leaving — His Arrest, His Obsession, The Closet

I finally left.
Packed my children.
Moved in with my mom.
Escaped.

Three days later, he came to my job—
stood in the lobby, patients waiting, coworkers watching.
He yelled,
"Bitch, bring your ass here!"

I yelled back,
"Leave before I call the police."

He said,
"I don't give a damn."

Later, he followed me again—
cornered me in an elevator,
bent my finger backward,
threatened me until someone called the police.

He was arrested.
I resigned from that job immediately.

After that, I didn't want to keep involving my mom.
So I went back home.

That's when he locked me in the closet
and told me he loved me so much.
Love twisted into control.
Obsession disguised as devotion.

The Crowbar Attack — The Final Break

One day, it started with something small—
a wallpaper on my phone.
The *Love Jones* movie wallpaper.
Not a man.
Just a wallpaper.

I was dropping him off for work with his brothers.
I left my kids with my sister.
The entire time, he kept accusing me—
twisting it into betrayal.

He got out of the car.
As I pulled off, he tried to jump back in.
I crashed the car.

After the crash, we were fighting.
I wasn't afraid of him then.
That's when he snapped and swung the crowbar.

Metal hit skin.
Pain exploded.
The world blurred.
I staggered,
blood rushing in my ears,
the weight of his rage pressing down on me.

I walked away and ended up on a stranger's doorstep.
A woman opened the door and called the police.
Her kindness was the first mercy I had felt in months.

I was crying,
a knot swelling on my head where he had hit me.

When the police arrived, they asked questions.
He told them I hit him, too.

An officer put me in the back of the police car.
I had never been in one before.
It felt strange.
Uncomfortable.
Wrong.

He yelled,
"Arrest that bitch. She scratched me."
He held up his arms, showing the scratches.

Witnesses spoke.
We were both taken to jail.

They released me on my own recognizance—
I had never been arrested before.

From across the room, he yelled,
"Baby, I'm sorry."

That's when I knew—
this man was obsessed.
This was not love.

But I was young.
And I was addicted to him—
to the intensity,
to the closeness,
to the way it felt like love at first sight.

That confusion kept me longer than it should have.

An officer whispered,
"If you don't leave him, he's going to kill you."

That night in a jail cell, I realized:
His insecurity almost cost me my life.
And if I stayed,
it would.

When My Son Stepped In the Last Straw

We were separated by then — not just in the legal sense, but in the
way two people become strangers long before the paperwork catches
up.
He came by to drop off money for our daughter, and for a moment,
the air felt almost neutral.
Not peaceful, but quiet enough to pretend.

Then my phone rang.
I smiled.
A small, harmless smile.
The kind you give when you recognize a ringtone or remember
something funny.

But in his mind, that smile belonged to another man.
Jealousy didn't simmer — it detonated.

Before I could inhale, he lunged.
He ripped the phone from my hand and slammed it against the wall.
The crack of glass echoed through the room like a warning shot.

Then he spit in my face — hot, sharp, humiliating.
"I hate you," he hissed.

The words didn't hurt as much as the look in his eyes.
There was no love left.
No respect.
Just something dark and unrecognizable.

My son — older now, taller, stronger — rose from the corner like a
storm forming.
His fists clenched.
His jaw locked.
His whole-body trembling with a rage he didn't ask for but felt
responsible to carry.

He stepped forward to defend me.

And in that instant, time slowed.
I saw two futures flash like lightning:
My son dying…
or my son going to jail…
all because he was trying to protect me from a man who should have
protected us both.

That moment should have been enough to make me walk away for
good.
But I didn't leave.
Not that day.
Not yet.

I was still tangled in the hope that maybe the worst had already
happened.
That maybe things would calm down.
That maybe I could hold the pieces together a little longer.
Hope can be a dangerous thing when you're surviving on it.

He carried a weight
that didn't belong to him.

A boy shouldn't have to monitor
a grown man's moods.
He shouldn't have to calculate
when to speak,
when to stay close,
or when to stand between his mother
and the storm she kept trying to outlove.

But he did.
Because he loved me.
Because he didn't trust the man I trusted.
Because he saw the truth
before I was ready to face it.

The day he finally spoke up,
it wasn't disrespect.
It was heartbreak.
A breaking point.

A moment where his fear
turned into a voice
he could no longer swallow.

He told me he was tired
of watching me hurt.
Tired of pretending everything was fine.
Tired of seeing me disappear
into someone else's chaos.

And hearing my own child
describe the version of me
I had become—
that was the moment
something inside me cracked open.

Not in shame.
In recognition.

He wasn't trying to control me.
He was trying to save me
from the parts of myself
that still believed endurance was love.

And that realization
shifted everything.

I stopped seeing him
as a child who didn't understand.
I saw him as the mirror
I had been avoiding.

The one person
who loved me enough
to tell the truth
without protecting my feelings.

The one person
who needed me to rise
so he could finally rest.

When My Nephews Found Out

Later that week, my nephew found out what happened — that this man spit in my face.
I didn't even finish the sentence before the air changed.
My nephews do not play with their aunt.
Their loyalty is loud.
Their love is fierce.
And when they heard what he did, the entire energy shifted.
It wasn't chaos.
It wasn't reckless.
It was clarity.
They didn't ask what I did.
They didn't question my story.
They didn't minimize the moment.
They didn't tell me to calm down or "let it go."
They stood up for me in a way I hadn't stood up for myself in a long time.
It wasn't about retaliation.
It was about respect.
It was about reminding me that I was worth defending.
That I wasn't alone.
That someone cared enough to say, "This is not okay."
Their reaction didn't fix the situation —
It fixed my vision.

What Shifted Inside Me

For years, I had carried everything quietly.
The disrespect.
The humiliation.
The slow erosion of my spirit.
I had convinced myself that enduring was the same as surviving.
That silence was strength.
That shrinking myself was the price of keeping the peace.
But when my family stepped in, something cracked open inside me.
A truth I had buried under years of trying to hold everything together

finally surfaced:

I deserved better.

My children deserved better.

My life deserved better.

Their outrage wasn't about anger —

It was about love.

It was about seeing me.

It was about reminding me of the woman I used to be before the chaos, before the fear, before the exhaustion.

Something shifted.

Something permanent.

And once that shift happened, there was no going back.

That week didn't just change my situation.

It changed me.

It was the beginning of the end —

and the beginning of my return to myself.

The Kiss That Pulled Me Back In

I didn't expect anything from that night. Weddings have a way of making people believe in things they've long stopped trusting—love, promises, forever—but I walked into his brother's ceremony with my guard high and my heart tucked away. I was there for the family, nothing more. At least that's what I told myself.

The room glowed with soft amber lights, the kind that make everything look warmer than it really is. Laughter floated through the air, champagne glasses clinked, and the DJ played those feel-good songs that make even the most broken hearts sway. I remember standing off to the side, trying to blend into the celebration, when I felt it—his eyes on me.

It wasn't a gentle glance. It was a pull. A familiar gravity I had spent months trying to escape.

When I finally looked up, our eyes locked across the room. Something in the atmosphere shifted, like the whole place inhaled at once. He started walking toward me—slow, steady, sure—and I didn't move. I didn't look away. I didn't even breathe.

By the time he reached me, the noise around us had blurred into a distant hum. And then it happened. That kiss. Sudden. Familiar. Heavy with history. It wasn't soft or tentative. It was the kind of kiss that drags you backward in time, straight into the version of yourself that once believed in the best parts of him.

For a moment, it felt like stepping into a memory I hadn't fully let go of.

But even as his hands pulled me closer, a quiet thought pressed against the back of my mind:
Am I doing this for us… or for her?

Because the truth is, I wanted my daughter to have a family that looked whole. I wanted her to see two parents standing on the same side of life, not opposite ends of a battlefield. I wanted stability for her, even if it meant sacrificing pieces of myself to create the illusion.

So I let the kiss happen. I let the moment swallow me. I let myself believe—just for a second—that maybe this time would be different. That maybe love could be rebuilt if I held on tight enough. That maybe choosing him again meant choosing something better for her.

And after that kiss, after that moment that felt like a doorway back into a life I wasn't sure I wanted—we made a decision that should have felt hopeful but instead felt heavy.

We decided to renew our wedding vows.

As if repeating the ceremony could rewrite the truth.
As if saying "I do" again could undo the damage.
As if a fresh promise could erase the old wounds.

Looking back, I know exactly what that kiss was: not a sign, not a miracle, not a second chance. It was a moment of longing dressed up as love. A moment where exhaustion felt like hope. A moment where

I tried to convince myself that the picture of family mattered more
than the reality of my peace.

But at the time, all I could feel was the pull.
The kiss that drew me back in.
The kiss that changed the direction of everything that came next.

Remarrying Him

Months later, I remarried him—
not out of love,
but hoping for stability for my daughter.

The truth is, we actually never got divorced;
it was more of a renewal.
People said,
"Oh, he loves you,"
but that was not love.

When we renewed our vows,
I knew deep down I was no longer connected.
My heart had already left,
even if my body stayed for a while.

Chaos always returns
to where it was never healed.

One day my son said,
"Mom... please. Let's go."

And in that moment,
his voice carried more truth than any vow,
more clarity than any promise,
more love than the man I had married twice.

The Truth Always Finds Its Way Out

We stayed together for only four months after the second wedding.
Four months of pretending the past didn't exist.
Four months of forcing a future that was already broken.
Four months of hoping love could hold together what life had
already broken apart.
But the truth doesn't knock.
It kicks the door open.
That's how I found out he had dated another woman during our
separation.
Not a rumor.
Not a misunderstanding.
A fact.
And the irony?
I had married him again while he was entertaining someone else.
But life has a strange way of balancing itself.
Because during that same time, I met someone else —
someone who would later become my husband.
We were doing well financially.
He had a good job.
I had been at my job for years.
For once, I wasn't choosing from survival.
My son didn't approve,
but he supported me.
And that kind of loyalty stays with you.
Those four months taught me more than the entire relationship ever
did.
Truth rises.
Love without honesty is performance.
And sometimes the person you're meant to be with doesn't show up
until you finally let go of the one who was holding you back.

The Call That Changed Everything

After I found out about the other woman,
I did something most women wouldn't do.
I talked to her.

Not out of jealousy —
out of clarity.
She told me everything.
He had told her we were never back together.
He had spoken badly about me.
He had rewritten our entire story.
So, we set him up on a three-way call.
He didn't know I was on the line.
She asked him:
"Did you and Corrina get married again?"
He paused.
Then said:
"No.
I do not want her."
The words sliced through me.
Not because I wanted him —
but because I had stayed with someone who didn't want me.
That call didn't break me.
It broke the illusion.
It ended my denial.
It freed me.

It wasn't anger.
It wasn't rebellion.
It was protection.
It was heartbreak.
It was the plea of a child
who had carried too much for too long.

I looked at him,
and I saw the weight he had carried—
the sleepless nights,
the silent calculations,
the fear he never spoke out loud.

Leaving wasn't just my decision anymore.
It was his salvation, too.
It was the moment I chose us,
chose freedom,
chose to finally walk away for good.

The First Morning of My New Life

One morning, after everything,
He left for work like it was any other day.
But it wasn't.
It was the day I decided I was done.
While he was gone,
I packed up my entire home.
Every drawer.
Every closet.
Every memory.
My kids helped me.
Their faces said everything —
relief, understanding, pride.
By sunset, the house was empty.
Silent.
Clean in a way that felt like closure.
I drove away with my kids and felt something I hadn't felt in years:
Freedom.

The Woman I Am Now

I am not who I was.
Not the woman who tolerated disrespect.
Not the woman who confused chaos with love.
Not the woman who lost herself trying to fix a broken man.

Healing washed the memories clean.
God rewrote my story.
I forgave him—not for him, but for me.

I am GOOD.
I am WHOLE.
I am HEALED.

What was meant to break me became the foundation of the woman I
am today:
A survivor.
A mother.
A fighter.
A woman of God.
A woman reborn.
A woman restored.

I did not deserve that kind of love.
I deserved better—and I became better.

CHAPTER 7
THE SPACE BETWEEN WHO I WAS AND WHO I WAS BECOMING

Leaving my first marriage didn't immediately heal me.
Survival is not the same as recovery. Freedom is not the same as
healing.
When I walked away from him, I was free —
but I was fractured.
I survived chaos, violence,
betrayal, loss, heartbreak,
and the kind of wounds that settle deep in your spirit long before you
notice they're bleeding.
And even though I left the man who almost destroyed me, I still
carried his impact inside me.

The Woman I Was After the Storm

I was tired —
not just physically,
but emotionally, mentally, spiritually.
I had two children looking at me for guidance.
A daughter who fought her way into this world
and a son who watched me survive more than any child should.
I was rebuilding myself
while trying to rebuild their trust in me. I was healing from:
• the miscarriages
• the verbal abuse
• the physical abuse
• the betrayal
• the sexual violence
• the financial instability
• the fear
• the shame
• the disappointment in myself

I didn't realize it then,
but I was grieving versions of myself I would never get back.
Before I could enter anything new, I had to feel everything old.
And I did.
I cried quietly.
I parented loudly.
I prayed deeply.
I worked hard.
I survived silently.
I rebuilt slowly.
I looked in the mirror and didn't recognize the woman staring back
— but I knew I had to create her.

The Man Who Entered During My Transition

It was during this fragile, in-between place
that I met the man who would become my second husband.
I didn't know it at the time,
but he wasn't sent by God —
He was sent by my brokenness.
Women don't always fall for better after leaving a bad man.
Sometimes, they fall for different.
And different can be just as dangerous.
He came in during the moment when my spirit was tired
and my heart was craving peace.
He came in when my guard was down, but my hope was still alive.
He came in when I was vulnerable, soft,
healing,
and trying to rebuild my sense of worth.
He felt like relief —
but he was a distraction.
A lesson.
A mirror showing me the wounds I hadn't healed yet.
The truth is:
I wasn't ready for love.
I wasn't ready for marriage.
I wasn't even ready for partnership.
I was still bleeding.

And he stepped into the doorway of my healing with a smile,
soft words,
and intentions I didn't know yet would hurt me
in ways my first husband never did.
The stage was set.
The healing was incomplete. The heart was open.
The spirit was tired.
And the next chapter of my life was about to begin —
not because I was ready for it,
but because the lesson had to be lived before it could be learned.

CHAPTER 8

THE PERFECT PRETENDER — AND THE LIFE THAT SAVED ME

When God rescues you from a storm, you expect sunlight.
You expect warmth.
You expect rest.

You don't expect the enemy to send a man who feels like shade—
cool, calming, and deadly.

He didn't come with chaos.
He came with quiet.
With softness.
With the kind of patience that makes a broken woman exhale for the
first time in years.

He studied my wounds like a map.
He learned the places I ached.
He learned the places I blamed myself.
He learned the places I still believed I deserved less.
And then he used every one of them.

I thought he was peaceful because he wasn't yelling.
I thought he was in love because he wasn't hitting.
I thought he was safe because he wasn't my first husband.

But predators don't always roar.
Sometimes they whisper.
Sometimes they hold your hand while they lead you straight into hell.

I was fresh out of trauma—bleeding, exhausted, desperate for
softness.
And he knew it.
He smelled it on me like smoke after a fire.

What I thought was healing was really a setup.
A counterfeit blessing dressed in everything I thought I lacked.
A man who mirrored my needs just long enough to get close enough
to destroy me.

I wasn't stepping into love.
I was stepping into another storm—
one that didn't announce itself with thunder,
one that almost took my life with silence.

He Entered My Life Like a Familiar Face with a Different Agenda

I met him in a club—dim lights, slow music, people laughing like life
had never cut them open.
He looked familiar in a way that made my spirit pause.
Later I learned he'd been friends with my cousin for years.
But that night, he was just a beautiful distraction with red-toned skin,
soft curls braided back, bow-legged confidence, and a face fine
enough to make a woman forget her boundaries.

He liked that I didn't smoke.
He liked that I didn't drink.
He said it made me "different."
And back then, I held onto anything that made me feel chosen.

But I *was* different.
I was stronger.
I had a voice now—one I fought to reclaim after surviving a man
who tried to erase me.
He told me he was used to insecure women, women who didn't
speak up, women who didn't challenge him.
And instead of hearing the warning in that, I took it as a compliment.

Now I look back and ask myself:
If he was used to insecure women… why did I end up with him?
What part of me thought I could be the exception?

What part of me ignored the red flags because he was fine and I had
a weakness for fine men back then?

But it wasn't just his looks.
I think I loved that he didn't just want me for sex.
He complimented my beauty and my intelligence—
like he saw the woman I was trying to grow into.
And I complimented him too.
We fed each other's egos, each other's wounds, each other's need to
feel valued.
We complimented each other in all the ways that feel good at first
but turn dangerous when you confuse validation with love.

He became my best friend.
The person I laughed with.
The person I confided in.
The person who made the world feel a little less heavy.

And maybe that's where I went wrong.
I should've left it at friendship.
I should've never touched the commitment part.
Because the moment feelings got involved, the moment I let my
guard down,
everything shifted.

What felt like comfort became confusion.
What felt like safety became another storm.
And I didn't realize it until I was already drowning in it.

A Warning from the Dead

The day before my cousin was murdered,
he looked me dead in my eyes and said,
"Cuz… that man is NOT for you."

It wasn't casual.
It wasn't small talk.
It wasn't one of those warnings people throw out just to be heard.

It was a plea.
A truth spoken with urgency,
from someone who knew him better than I ever wanted to admit.

Because my cousin wasn't just family—
he was his friend.
They laughed together.
Shared secrets.
Shared time I was never part of.
He knew the version of that man I hadn't met yet.
The one behind the charm.
The one behind the mask.

So, when he spoke,
it wasn't rumor.
It wasn't jealousy.
It wasn't interference.
It was proximity.
It was insight.
It was love trying to protect me.

And that's what made the warning cut deeper.
He actually liked him.
But he still told me the truth.

His voice still echoes in my spirit.
A warning from God,
delivered by someone who wouldn't live to repeat it.
Even in death,
he tried to save me.
And I wish I had listened.

Because now I see—
that warning wasn't just his.
It was ancestral.
It was divine.
It was every part of my intuition trying to shake me awake.

But I was too entangled.
Too hopeful.

Too afraid to start over again.
So I silenced the voice that was trying to protect me.
And in silencing it,
I picked up a regret I would carry for years.

Now, when I think back,
I don't just grieve his death.
I grieve the version of me who ignored his wisdom.
The woman who wanted love so badly
she walked past a warning delivered by blood.

And yet, his words still live inside me.
They remind me to trust my intuition.
To honor the voices that speak truth.
To never again dismiss the warnings—
even when they come softly,
even when they come from the dead.

The On-and-Off Cycle — A Warning I Ignored

After the warning from the dead,
after my cousin tried to reach me from the other side,
life didn't fall apart all at once.

It started with patterns.
Cycles.
Repeating lessons I refused to learn.

From the very beginning, we were unstable.
Break up.
Make up.
Repeat.

A rhythm so familiar it almost felt like home.

During one of our "breaks," he even married another woman.
People whispered.
Rumors floated back to me like smoke.

But I stayed quiet—
too used to swallowing pain,
too tired to chase truth that was already hurting me.

And every time our paths crossed,
that spark lit up again.
Not love—
just history mixed with loneliness,
the kind of pull that feels like fate when you're still healing.

But it wasn't fate.
It was a trauma bond wearing a soulmate's mask.

Looking back, I can see it clearly:
the warning had already started.
My cousin tried to tell me.
My spirit tried to tell me.
But I kept choosing the familiar over the truthful.

The truth is, I wanted him because I was holding on to the
friendship.
Holding on to the good moments.
Holding on to the parts of our connection that felt warm
when everything else in my life felt cold.

I kept choosing the positive pieces
and ignoring the damage underneath them.

And my kids loved him.
They really did.
And no matter how the story ends,
I will always say he was good to them.
That part was real.
That part mattered.

Eventually, we moved in together,
convincing ourselves that closeness could fix
what distance never healed.

But I didn't know it then—
I wasn't walking into stability.
I was walking deeper into the very warning I had ignored.

The signs were there.
The energy was shifting.
The ancestors had already spoken.

And I was about to learn
what happens when you ignore a message
that was sent to save you.

The Day Everything Snapped (Before Marriage)

We were living together but living apart—two strangers sharing the
same space, pretending the silence between us wasn't swallowing us
whole.
Something in me had already shifted. Something in him had already
drifted.

One day, my spirit grew restless.
Not anxious—*aware*.
A quiet warning rising up from a place I had learned to trust.

I left the house and followed that feeling straight to his car… parked
outside another woman's home.
The same woman he swore was "family," someone connected to his
so-called nephew.
My intuition didn't whisper.
It demanded: *Check*.

So, I did.
I used my spare key and got into his car.
His Nextel sat on the seat like a confession waiting to be heard.
Then it rang.

A woman's voice came through, bold and comfortable:
"He must be somewhere drunk, because he doesn't let NOBODY
get to that phone."

My heart didn't just drop—it cracked open.
If this was my man, why did I suddenly feel like the other woman?
Why did she sound more certain of him than I ever felt?

We ended up arguing in the middle of the street.
Voices raised.
Pain exposed.
Neighbors watching like it was entertainment.

Then the police pulled up.
And the officer stepping out was someone I went to school with.
He looked at me—really looked—and said,
"Corrina… this is not you."

His words hit me like a flashback.
Another reminder of who I used to be.
Another reminder of how far I had fallen from myself.
And instead of breaking down, I got angry.
Angry at him.
Angry at the situation.
Angry at myself for being in a place where someone had to remind
me of my own identity.

That moment should've been my exit.
That was God handing me the door.
But unhealed women stay in places healed women wouldn't even step
into.
And I stayed—carrying sorrow I didn't yet recognize,
holding onto a man who had already let go of me.

The Christmas Proposal

Two months before our wedding —
not long enough to truly know a person,

but long enough for the truth to start whispering —
he proposed.

It was Christmas.
A holiday meant for warmth, family, and intention.
But nothing about that moment felt intentional.

There was no planning.
No buildup.
No conversation about our future.
No moment where he looked at me with certainty or love.

Just a rushed proposal wrapped in holiday noise.

Before he even asked me,
he pulled my son aside —
my baby, my protector, my little man who only wanted to see his
mother happy —
and asked him if he could take my hand in marriage.

And of course, my son said yes.
Because the man he saw then
was not abusive,
not deceitful,
not dangerous.
He saw a man who smiled,
who played the part,
who pretended to be gentle and trustworthy.

My son saw the version of him that *I* once believed in.

He didn't see the lies.
He didn't see the secrets.
He didn't see the storm that was coming.

A moment that should've felt like forever
ended up being the first sign
that forever was never meant for us.

A Courthouse Marriage My Mother Didn't Approve

Two months after that rushed Christmas proposal,
I found myself standing in a courthouse —
not in a gown,
not with flowers,
not with music or family or celebration…

Just me, him, and a decision I wasn't ready to make.

And guess what?
We were married on Friday, February 13th.
A date people avoid.
A date that should've told me everything.

Even now, I still ask myself:
Why was he rushing?
Why did it have to be *that* day?
Why did it feel like he was racing against a truth I hadn't discovered
yet?

I didn't wear a wedding dress.
But my outfit?
On point.
Sharp.
Stylish.
Put together.

On the outside, I looked ready.
But inside, I was falling apart.

And the whole time, a voice in my head kept whispering,
"What am I thinking?"

My mom was so upset with me.
Not because she didn't love me —
but because she *did*.
Because she had raised me with standards,

with dignity,
with the belief that marriage was sacred and intentional.

And I valued her opinion most of the time.
But not that day.
That day, I ignored her.
I ignored myself.
I ignored every warning God whispered to me.

I walked into that courthouse with a knot in my stomach so tight it
felt like a fist.
Something in me knew I shouldn't be there.
Something in me knew this wasn't my wedding —
it was my surrender.

There was no joy.
No excitement.
No butterflies.
Just a quiet heaviness sitting on my chest.

He stood beside me smiling,
acting like this was the beginning of forever,
while I stood there feeling like I was signing away pieces of myself.

The judge read the vows.
We repeated the words.
We exchanged rings.
And just like that,
I was a wife.

But I didn't feel married.
I felt trapped.

When we walked out of the courthouse,
there was no celebration.
No family waiting.
No pictures.
No moment to cherish.

Just silence.

My mother didn't speak to me for days.
Not out of anger —
but out of heartbreak.
She had raised me to know better,
to choose better,
to listen to my intuition.

And I had ignored all of it.

I told myself it was love.
I told myself it was timing.
I told myself it was destiny.

But deep down, I knew the truth:

I didn't walk into that courthouse because I was in love.
I walked in because I was afraid of starting over.
Afraid of being alone.
Afraid of admitting I had made a mistake.

That courthouse wedding wasn't the beginning of our marriage.
It was the beginning of my silence.
The beginning of me shrinking myself.
The beginning of me abandoning my own voice.

And the saddest part?
I didn't realize then
that the woman who walked out of that courthouse
was already disappearing.

The Reception — The First Sign I Ignored

We had a reception the next day.
A damn thrown-together reception my mother did **not** approve of.
She took one look around and whispered under her breath,
"This is ghetto."
And she meant it.

My mother was bougie, classy, and prideful—
the kind of woman who believed in linen tablecloths, real
centerpieces,
and events that matched the dignity she raised me with.
So standing in that room, surrounded by chaos disguised as
celebration,
I could feel her disappointment without her saying another word.

Family and friends gathered, smiling, celebrating,
trying to make the best of something I already felt uneasy about.

I moved through the room like a woman pretending—
pretending this was joy,
pretending this was love,
pretending I wasn't already questioning everything inside me.

Then one of his friends pulled me aside.
No hesitation.
No softness.
Just a blunt truth delivered like a slap:

"You're a fool for marrying him."

It hit me so hard I felt the floor tilt.
My stomach dropped.
My spirit tightened.

And before I could even process it, chaos erupted.

My husband and that same friend were suddenly in a full-blown
brawl—
loud, violent, reckless.
A knife flashed.
Instinct took over.
I reached in to stop it, and pain shot through my hand as the blade
sliced me.

Blood.
Chaos.
Humiliation.

My wedding reception turned into a crime scene.
Guests screaming.
Security rushing in.
And me—standing there with blood dripping down my arm,
wondering how my life had spiraled into this.

I ended up in the hospital.
We were kicked out of the hotel.

And all I could think was:
This is my wedding day.
This is my husband.
This is my life now.

I was wounded—physically and emotionally.
Embarrassed.
Drowning in regret I didn't yet have the courage to name.

And then—
the very same day we were married—
he went to the club with his boys.

No concern.
No apology.
No accountability.
Just abandonment dressed up as a celebration.

I wanted to run.
Wanted to disappear.
Wanted to undo every decision that led me to that moment.

But I didn't want to hear the words I feared most:
"I told you so."

So I stayed.
And sadness became my silent companion—
the shadow that followed me everywhere,
the weight I carried alone.

Living With Marriage — The Disrespect Began Quietly

The first days of marriage are supposed to feel different—
softer, safer, sacred.
But nothing changed for me.
If anything, things got worse.

He didn't ease into disrespect.
He slid into it like it was home.

At first, it was the late nights.
Hours passing with no call, no text, no explanation.
I'd sit in the living room with the TV on mute,
listening for the sound of his car,
listening for footsteps that never came when they should have.

He'd walk in at three, four, sometimes five in the morning,
smelling like outside,
eyes glazed,
clothes wrinkled,
attitude sharp.

No apology.
No accountability.
Just a shrug, a lie, or worse—silence.

And I'd stand there,
a new wife with a fresh wound on her hand,
wondering how I went from a wedding ring
to feeling single in my own home.

The disrespect grew slowly,
like mold in the corners of a room you stop paying attention to.

He stopped answering his phone.
Stopped coming home after work.
Stopped caring if I asked where he'd been.

He'd leave the house dressed like he was auditioning for attention—
fresh haircut, new clothes, cologne so strong it walked in before he
did.
And I'd watch him walk out the door
knowing damn well he wasn't going anywhere that required a wife.

He started talking to me like I was a burden.
Like my questions were disrespect.
Like my presence was an inconvenience.

And the worst part?
He acted like this was normal.
Like this was marriage.
Like I should just accept it.

But I wasn't raised like that.
I was raised by a woman who believed in standards,
in dignity,
in being treated with respect.

Yet here I was—
a wife in name only,
living with a man who treated the streets better than he treated me.

Nights turned into patterns.
Patterns turned into routine.
And routine turned into a truth I didn't want to face:

I wasn't married to a partner.
I was married to a ghost—
a man who lived everywhere except home,
who gave his time to everyone except me,
who respected everything except our marriage.

And every time he walked out that door,
a little piece of me walked out with him.

But I stayed.
Because I didn't want to admit the truth.
Because I didn't want to face the embarrassment.

Because I didn't want to hear the words I feared most:
"I told you so."

So I swallowed the disrespect.
I swallowed the loneliness.
I swallowed the pain.

And that's how the marriage began—
with me shrinking,
and him disappearing,
both of us living under the same roof
but in completely different worlds.

A Season of Elevation — When Everything Looked Like It Was Finally Working

There was a time—before the storms, before the disrespect, before the unraveling—when life with him actually felt good.
A time when we were moving forward, building, dreaming, and believing we were stepping into something better.

After everything we had been through, the idea of a fresh start felt like oxygen.
So we opened our own business.
And for a while, it worked.

Money was coming in.
Clients were steady.
We were building something together, something that felt like purpose, like partnership, like progress.
And for the first time in a long time, I felt proud of us.
Proud of what we were creating.
Proud of the momentum we had.

Then came the opportunity that changed everything:
Las Vegas.

A new city.
A new beginning.
A new federal job for me—steady, respectable, secure.
It felt like God was giving us a reset button.

We sold everything.
Packed up our lives.
And drove across the country with hope riding in the backseat.

The moment we arrived in Vegas, the air felt different.
Lighter.
Open.
Full of possibility.

The city was alive—bright lights, warm nights, endless opportunity.
And for a while, we matched that energy.
We were laughing more.
Working more.
Dreaming more.

Our business started elevating in ways we hadn't imagined.
New clients.
New contracts.
New money.
We were building a name for ourselves, and it felt good—really good.

We traveled all the time, especially to California.
Quick trips.
Weekend getaways.
Business mixed with pleasure.
It felt like freedom.
Like we were finally living instead of surviving.

There were moments on those drives—windows down, music up,
desert sun hitting the car—when I looked over at him and thought,
Maybe we made it. Maybe this is our turning point.

For a season, we were aligned.
Focused.

Motivated.
Moving in the same direction.

And I won't lie—
that season mattered.
It was real.
It was ours.
And it's important to tell the truth about it.

Because before everything fell apart,
before the disrespect,
before the betrayal,
before the heartbreak that nearly broke me—
there was a time when we were rising.

A time when I believed in us.
A time when I believed in him.
A time when I believed in the future we were building.

And maybe that's why the fall hurt so much.
Because I knew what we were capable of.
I had seen the best of him.
I had seen the potential of us.

There was a time when everything looked like it was finally working
A time when life felt full, hopeful, and promising.

A time when I truly thought we were going to win.

Las Vegas: The Weight I Carried

Months later, we moved to Las Vegas.
Packed up our entire lives.
Sold everything.
Left behind every comfort, every routine, every piece of stability I
had built on my own.

It felt like a fresh start—
a new chapter,
a chance to rebuild something stronger than the mess we had created.

We opened businesses.
We had big dreams.
We made plans that looked good on paper.

But paper can't hold truth.

And the truth was this:
I was pulling all the weight.

Every idea.
Every plan.
Every dollar.
Every sacrifice.
Mine.

And the part that stings the most?

He knew exactly who I was.
He knew I was smart.
He knew I was business-savvy.
He knew I was a warrior—
the kind of woman who doesn't fold,
doesn't quit,
doesn't crumble under pressure.

And he used that.

He leaned on my strength because he had none of his own.
He hid behind my hustle.
He used my resilience as his safety net.
He let me carry the load while he coasted on the life I built.

I wasn't his partner.
I was his lifeline.
His stability.

His structure.
His cover.

And I didn't realize it then,
but Las Vegas wasn't a fresh start.
It was the beginning of the end—
the place where the truth finally became too heavy to ignore.

When the Past Wouldn't Let Us Live

For a moment, it looked like we were finally living life.
We met new friends.
We went out more.
We tried to build something that looked normal from the outside.
I tried to convince myself we were moving forward.

But he couldn't leave our past behind.
No matter how much I tried to grow, he stayed the same.
Still entertaining women from Baltimore.
Still dipping back into old habits, old conversations, old connections
that should've died the day he chose me.

It didn't matter how many new people we met.
It didn't matter how many fresh starts we tried to create.
His past was always sitting in the room with us—
loud, messy, and uninvited.

And every time I found out he was still entertaining those women,
it felt like a slap from the universe saying,
"You knew who he was."

I was trying to build a future with a man who kept running back to
the same doors he claimed he had closed.
And no matter how much I wanted us to move forward,
he kept dragging us backward.

That was the truth I didn't want to face:
I was fighting for a version of him that never existed.

The Baby That Exposed Everything

It wasn't a phone call.
It wasn't a confession.
It wasn't even a rumor whispered through the grapevine.

It was Facebook.

A random scroll.
A normal day.
A moment that should've meant nothing.

Until it meant everything.

I wasn't looking for anything.
I wasn't snooping.
I wasn't digging.
I was just living—trying to hold together a marriage that was already slipping through my fingers.

Then my inbox lit up.

A message request.
A name I didn't recognize.
A young lady messaged me out of nowhere, saying she needed to share something with me…
she had a baby by my husband.

Her words were calm, almost gentle—
like she was trying to soften a blow that was already breaking me open.

She told me her son was four.
Four.
Not newborn.
Not recent.
Four.

My stomach dropped.
My hands went cold.
My world tilted.

Then she sent the picture.

The moment I saw that child's face,
my stomach dropped all over again.
He was his twin.
Same eyes.
Same expression.
There was no denying it.

This wasn't just a secret.
This wasn't just a lie.
This was a life—
a whole child—
hidden from me for years.

When I confronted him,
he lied without blinking.
Told me he had no idea.
Told me he didn't know anything about a child.

But the woman had receipts.
So many that it was embarrassing to even talk about.
Messages.
Dates.
Pictures.
Proof.

And the worst part?

I found out he had gone to the hospital when the baby was born.
Held the child.
Took pictures.
Played the proud father.
Then came home to me
like nothing happened.

In that moment,
I didn't feel like a wife.
I didn't feel like a partner.
I didn't feel chosen.
I felt like the side chick.

And now that I think about it,
everything makes sense.
The pressure.
The urgency.
The way he pushed so hard for us to move to Vegas.
He wasn't chasing a fresh start—
he was running.
Running from responsibility.
Running from exposure.
Running from the truth that was eventually going to find me anyway.

Facebook didn't break me.
Vegas didn't break us.
His truth did.

And once I saw who he really was,
I couldn't unsee it.
I couldn't understand it.
I couldn't pretend anymore.

The man I married never existed.
The man I loved was a mask.
The man I fought for was a lie.

And that baby—
that innocent child—
became the mirror that exposed everything I refused to see.

The HIV Revelation — The Moment My Soul Broke

After the fallout, after the lies, after the moment my heart detached and never returned, I thought I had already seen the worst of him. I thought the Facebook revelation was the final blow. I thought nothing else could break me any further.

But life has a way of showing you that rock bottom has a basement. And that's where this chapter begins.

The rumors came first — quiet, messy, whispered things that somehow felt louder than the truth I was living in. My cousin told me what she heard, and it shook me. She said people were saying he was HIV positive. I asked him about the allegations, and he got defensive — snapping, irritated, acting like my fear was an insult instead of a plea for honesty. That alone should've told me everything. And the thing is… He had already been tested before. Earlier in our marriage, he tested negative. Then again before his major surgery — another negative. Two clean tests. Two reassurances I trusted. So when the rumors resurfaced, something inside me tightened. A knot I couldn't ignore anymore. A knowing I didn't want to admit. I confronted him. He lied without flinching — like lying was muscle memory. Like, truth was optional. So we bought a home test from Walgreens and sat at the kitchen table where we once planned a future — the same table where we talked about dreams, bills, vacations, and kids. Now it held fear, silence, and two swabs that would change everything. We swabbed our saliva in complete silence.

Two swabs.

Two lives.

Two truths waiting to be exposed.

In less than two minutes,

his test turned positive.

Mine took almost forty minutes before the line appeared — negative.

The silence that followed was suffocating.

Thick.

Heavy.

Unforgiving.

It felt like the air itself was grieving.

He looked at me, eyes wide, voice trembling:

"Baby… what does this mean?"

His tone wasn't just fear.

It was disbelief.

Shock.

A man watching his world collapse in real time —

but I had already been living in the rubble.

I stared at the box, numb, and said,

"Let's call the number on the back."

We did.

The voice on the other end listened, then said plainly,

"This is accurate. You should go to Planned Parenthood for
confirmatory testing."

And in that moment, something inside me sank.

Because deep down, I already knew.

I wasn't surprised.

Not even a little.

We weren't sexually active as often as married couples usually are.

But back then, I didn't understand what that meant.

I didn't see the signs for what they were.

I didn't want to.

All I could see was the wreckage of my life scattered across that
kitchen table —

every lie,

every betrayal,

every ignored intuition,

every warning I silenced,

every moment, I chose hope over reality.

That night, he cried — sobbed like a child.

Begged.

Collapsed into himself.

He kept saying he didn't know how this happened,

kept asking me to hold him,

kept reaching for a comfort he no longer had access to.

And I sat there, frozen, hollow, numb.

Because this wasn't just a diagnosis.

It was the death of every dream I had for that marriage.

The death of the fantasy I kept trying to resurrect.

The death of the woman who kept choosing him over herself.

It was the moment I realized I had been loyal to a lie.

And yet… I prayed.

I prayed that night because I didn't want him to have HIV —

even though I didn't love him anymore.

Even though he had broken me in ways I hadn't even processed yet.

Even though he had risked my life without hesitation.

That prayer wasn't for him.

It was for the version of me who still believed love could fix what
truth had already destroyed.

A man I once thought I loved so deeply,

a man who was once my desire,

was now a stranger to my heart.

And now he has HIV.

And in that moment,

I realized something painful and undeniable:

love wasn't enough to save us,

and God was showing me the exit I had been too afraid to take.

The Disconnect When My Heart Left Before I Did

After the HIV revelation, something inside me shifted.
Not loudly.
Not dramatically.
But permanently.

My heart left before my body ever did.

I moved through the house like a ghost — present, but not alive.
I cooked.
I cleaned.
I worked.
I smiled when I had to.
But inside, I was gone.

He tried to act normal, like nothing had happened.
Like the truth, it hadn't shattered the foundation of our marriage.
Like we could just sweep betrayal under the rug and pretend it wasn't
bleeding through the floor.

But I couldn't unsee what I saw.
I couldn't unknow what I knew.
I couldn't unfeel the moment my soul broke at that kitchen table.

Every time he walked past me, I felt the distance grow.
Every time he touched me, my body stiffened.
Every time he said, "I love you," it felt like a lie echoing in an empty
room.

I wasn't angry anymore.
I wasn't even sad.
I was numb — the kind of numb that comes after too much pain,
too many lies, too many warnings ignored.

And he felt it.
He felt me slipping away.

He felt the silence.
He felt the shift.

But instead of accountability, he gave me guilt.
Instead of honesty, he gave me excuses.
Instead of healing, he gave me more reasons to leave.

I started sleeping on the edge of the bed.
Started staying up later.
Started waking up earlier.
Started finding peace in places he wasn't.

I didn't recognize myself anymore.
And I didn't recognize the man I married.

The truth was simple:
I wasn't his wife anymore.
I was his caretaker.
His cover.
His comfort.
His shield from consequences.

And I was tired.

Tired of carrying secrets that weren't mine.
Tired of protecting a man who never protected me.
Tired of shrinking myself to fit inside a marriage that was already
dead.

This was the chapter where I stopped fighting for us
and started fighting for me.

I didn't leave yet —
but the woman who once loved him was already gone.

Planned Parenthood — The Day Fear Took Over My Body

Before going to the health department, I went to Planned Parenthood —
terrified, confused, and desperate for answers.

The nurse took one look at me and said,
"You're safe here. Let's take care of you."

She didn't rush me.
She didn't judge me.
She just guided me gently to the back.

She asked softly,
"Why are you crying?"

And all I could whisper was,
"Just hurt... disappointed... all of the above."

She paused, looked straight into my eyes, and said something I will never forget:
"I can tell by your eyes you're a good person."

Then she added,
"No worries. Let's pray."

And she prayed with me —
not my norm, but I went with it,
because in that moment I needed something bigger than fear,
bigger than confusion,
bigger than the storm I was standing in.

She took my hands, bowed her head, and prayed over me like she had known me my whole life.
Her voice was steady, warm, and full of faith — the kind of faith I didn't have the strength to hold for myself.

Then she did a finger stick.
It took seconds.
But the waiting felt endless.

When the results came back,
my second HIV test was negative.
It felt good —
a wave of relief washing over me —
but I still didn't feel right.

Fear was still sitting in my chest.
My mind was still racing.
My spirit was still unsettled.

She reassured me again,
told me to breathe,
told me I was covered,
told me God had me even when I didn't feel held.

And in that moment —
in that tiny exam room with fluorescent lights and trembling hands

I felt something I hadn't felt in days:

Hope.

The Silent Ride Waiting for Confirmation

After Planned Parenthood, I still felt uneasy.
My body was calm, but my spirit wasn't.
Something in me knew the storm wasn't over.

The next morning, he suddenly wanted to drive me to work —
something he never did.
Not once.
Not before.
Not after.

The moment I sat in that passenger seat,
the air shifted.
Thick.
Heavy.
Unspoken.

He gripped the steering wheel like he was holding on for dear life.
I stared out the window,
trying to breathe through the knot in my stomach.

Neither of us said much.
But the silence said everything.

I kept replaying the nurse's words in my head:
"You're covered. God has you."
And I held onto that like a lifeline.

But fear still sat in my chest like a stone.

He kept glancing at me,
like he wanted to confess something
but didn't have the courage.

By the time we reached my job,
I felt like I had aged ten years.

I opened the door, stepped out,
and whispered a prayer under my breath:

"God… please don't let this be my ending."

I didn't know what the health department would say.
I didn't know what truth was waiting for me.
I didn't know what my life would look like in the next 24 hours.

All I knew was that something was coming —
and I could feel it in my bones.

This was the ride where my heart left the marriage
long before my body did.

The Weight of Staying — When Love Turned into Obligation

After the planned parenthood visit, after the tears, after the truth
settled into the walls of our home like a cold draft, something inside
me shifted permanently.
The marriage didn't end that day—
but *I* did.

I stayed for 2 weeks, but not out of love.
I stayed because I didn't know how to leave without breaking
completely.
I stayed because I didn't want the world to say,
"See? We told you."
I stayed because I was ashamed.
Ashamed of the choices I made.
Ashamed of the warnings I ignored.
Ashamed of the woman I had become.

Our house was stressful—
heavy with tension,
thick with silence,
filled with a sadness that clung to the walls like smoke.
Every room felt tight.
Every day felt long.
Every breath felt borrowed.

He walked around the house like a man carrying a secret he could no
longer hide.
Quiet.
Withdrawn.
Afraid.
And somehow, even in his fear, he still found ways to make me feel
guilty—
as if his diagnosis was a burden *we* shared,
as if I owed him comfort,
as if my heartbreak was an inconvenience.

I became the caretaker of a man who had never cared for me.
The emotional support for someone who had emotionally abandoned
me long before the truth came out.
The wife in name only—
but not in trust, not in intimacy, not in spirit.

Nights were the hardest.
He would cry,
and I would sit there,
staring at the wall,
feeling nothing.
Not anger.
Not sympathy.
Just emptiness.

I wasn't cold.
I was broken.

I prayed every night—
not for the marriage,
not for reconciliation,
but for strength.
Strength to survive the days.
Strength to protect my children.
Strength to find myself again.

And God heard me—
even when I didn't know what to ask for.
Even when I didn't have the courage to leave.
Even when I didn't recognize my own voice in prayer.

Because in the end,
he answered my prayer by leaving.

I started noticing things I had ignored before.
The way he avoided eye contact.
The way he flinched when his phone buzzed.
The way he tried to control the narrative—
as if rewriting the story could erase the truth.

But the truth was louder than both of us.

I wasn't his wife anymore.
I was his shield.
His cover.
His comfort.
His excuse.

And the weight of staying felt heavier than the fear of leaving.

This was the chapter where I realized something painful and
undeniable:
I could survive heartbreak, but I couldn't survive losing myself.

And even though I hadn't packed a single bag,
even though I hadn't spoken a single word about leaving,
my spirit was already walking toward the door.

The Final Betrayal — When He Left

The next two days, I went to work like nothing was wrong, even
though everything inside me was unraveling. I hadn't heard from him
at all. Not a text. Not a call. Nothing.

Then, around 1 p.m., my phone rang.

His voice was calm, almost relieved, when he said,
"I granted your request. I left."

I didn't understand at first.
Then it hit me—
he took *my* vehicle
and left the state.

By the time he called, he was already in Texas, driving.
We lived in Las Vegas.
He didn't just leave the house.
He left the entire state... in my car.

I cried, but not because he left.
I wasn't upset about losing him.
I had already detached long before that moment.

I cried because everything felt like chaos crashing down at once.
My life was spinning, and I couldn't catch my breath.

Minutes after his call, the phone rang again.
The health department.
They needed me to come in for more testing.

I was hysterically shaking, crying, unable to drive.
A coworker had to take me.
On the way, I told her everything, the words tumbling out between sobs.

When I arrived, I learned even more about HIV—
things I never wanted to know,
things no wife should ever have to learn this way.

They tested me again.
And then came the hardest part—
waiting.

A week of nervous nights.
A week of racing thoughts.
A week of whispered prayers, begging God to spare me.

Finally, the results came back:
Negative for everything.
God is so good.

My life changed after that moment.
But the betrayal didn't stop there.

When he left, he didn't just walk away.
He pawned all of our belongings and left the receipt on the bed.
I was devastated. That was his payback.

He left me with the wreckage.
He left me with the mess.
He left me with the truth.

And somehow, even in all that pain,
God still protected me.

Fourteen Years of Me — Learning to Live Without Love

Fourteen years.
Fourteen years of silence, healing, rebuilding, and rediscovering myself.
Fourteen years of learning what peace feels like after surviving a storm that almost took me out.

People think time heals everything.
But time doesn't heal —
truth does.
Distance does.
Choosing yourself does.

In those fourteen years, I learned how to breathe again.
How to sleep without fear.
How to wake up without anxiety sitting on my chest.
How to enjoy my own company without feeling lonely.

I dated lightly.
Laughed.
Went out.
Had fun.
But nothing serious.
Nothing that required me to hand over pieces of myself I had fought too hard to reclaim.

Because I finally understood the difference between
attention and intention.

Between someone wanting access to me
and someone deserving space in my life.

I learned how to protect my peace like it was oxygen.
How to trust my intuition the first time.
How to listen to the whispers God sends before they turn into
storms.

Fourteen years taught me that solitude isn't punishment.
It's protection.
It's clarity.
It's healing.

I didn't spend those years waiting for love.
I spent them **becoming** love.
Becoming whole.
Becoming the woman I needed when I was breaking.

I built a life.
A career.
A purpose.
A home filled with peace instead of chaos.
A heart filled with gratitude instead of fear.

My daughter grew into a woman I admire.
My son became a man I'm proud of.
And I kept my promise to them —
the cycle ended with me.

Fourteen years didn't make me bitter.
They made me better.
Wiser.
Softer in the right places, stronger in the ones that matter.

I didn't lose love.
I found myself.

And the woman I am today?
She is the proof that survival isn't the end of the story —
it's the beginning of becoming.

Becoming Myself Again — The Woman I Found in the Silence

After he left, after the chaos settled, after the fear loosened its grip on my chest, I stepped into a life I didn't recognize.
A life without him.
A life without constant worry.
A life without walking on eggshells.
A life without betrayal breathing down my neck.

At first, the silence felt strange.
Unfamiliar.
Too quiet.
Too still.

But slowly, that silence became my sanctuary.

I didn't rush into anything.
Not love.
Not dating.
Not commitment.
I didn't have the energy to rebuild with someone else when I was still rebuilding myself.

So, I stayed single.

And in that space, I found pieces of me I didn't even know I had lost.

I learned how to enjoy my own company.
How to sit with my thoughts without drowning in them.
How to laugh again without forcing it.
How to breathe without fear tightening my lungs.

I learned how to trust myself.
How to listen to my intuition.
How to honor the voice I had silenced for too long.

I dated here and there, but nothing serious.
Not because I was afraid —
but because I was finally discerning.
Finally aware.
Finally, I was unwilling to settle for anything that felt familiar in the wrong way.

I wasn't looking for love.
I was looking for peace.

And for the first time in my adult life,
I had it.

Fourteen years passed, and I didn't even realize how much time had gone by.
Because I wasn't waiting.
I wasn't longing.
I wasn't searching.

I was living.

I built a life that didn't require a partner to feel complete.
I built stability with my own hands.
I built joy from scratch.
I built a home filled with peace instead of tension.
I built a version of myself that didn't need saving.

And somewhere along the way, I realized something powerful:

I didn't lose love.
I found myself.

The woman I am today is not the woman who begged for loyalty.
Not the woman who ignored red flags.
Not the woman who stayed out of fear or shame.

I became a woman who chooses herself first.
A woman who knows her worth.
A woman who understands that solitude is not punishment —
it's protection.

Fourteen years didn't make me hard.
They made me whole.

CHAPTER 9

LOVED BY BLOOD, BETRAYED BY WOMEN

People love to romanticize sisterhood as if it's guaranteed—
as if every woman who shares your last name or your childhood
is automatically supposed to become love, support, and safety.

Life taught me something different.

Some of the deepest cuts I ever felt came from women who shared
my bloodline—
and later, from women who called me friend but violated the
meaning of the word.

People love to say, *"Family comes first."*
But what happens when the very women who share your blood
are the first ones to make you feel unwelcome?
What happens when the cousins who should've been your first
friends
become your first frenemies?

Growing up, I expected unity.
I expected closeness.
I expected love.

Instead, I walked into rooms and felt tension before I ever heard
hello.
I showed up with open arms—
they showed up with whispers, side-eyes, and fake smiles.

I heard things like:
"She thinks she's too cute."
"She thinks she's better."
"She thinks she's a superstar."

And when someone finally said it to my face,
my answer was simple and honest:

"I sure am."

Because if my confidence offends you,
your insecurity is the real issue.

One man even told me,
"Your cousin said, 'She wears makeup.'"

I laughed inside because... that was the big reveal?
Makeup?

Baby, the man didn't care.
If anything, she exposed her jealousy more than she exposed
anything about me.

It was never my makeup.
Never my clothes.
Never my confidence.

It was my **light**—
the way I carried myself with grace even when they prayed I would
fall.

It was my **honesty**—
my refusal to play along with secrets, denial, and generational
dysfunction.

That's why they labeled me the problem.
Not because I did anything wrong—
but because I was real in a family that survived by pretending.

The Phrase That Freed Me

One phrase followed me for years:

"Nobody wants her around."

At first, it stung.
Then it settled.
Then it freed me.

Because I stayed away—
not out of bitterness,
but out of wisdom.

I protected my energy.
Guarded my peace.
Chose distance over dysfunction.

They didn't dislike me because I was wrong.
They disliked me because I was **strong**.

Strong in a family that worshipped insecurity.
Bold in a family that hid behind silence.
Honest in a family where denial was tradition.

My spirit was too loud for their comfort.
My shine was too bright for their jealousy.
My truth was too sharp for their lies.

So I let them go.
And I've been thriving ever since.

Sisterhood That Was Really Competition

Then there was the one who called me "sis."
She spoke the language of sisterhood but moved like a rival.

Every success I shared became her battlefield.
If I published something, she rushed to outdo it.
If I celebrated a milestone, she tried to shrink it.

Her smile was wide—
but her eyes carried envy.

Her hugs were warm—
but her intentions were cold.

What I thought was support
was competition disguised as love.

She didn't want to grow with me—
she wanted to outrun me.
She didn't want to clap for me—
she wanted to drown out my applause.
She didn't want sisterhood—
she wanted a stage.

Some people don't want you to rise.
They want you to stay small so they can feel tall.

Friends Who Resented My Freedom

I remember a friend who grew upset with me simply because I was
single.
Not lonely.
Not searching.
Not settling.

Single—
and enjoying it.

I could hear it in her tone.
See it in her reactions.
Feel it in the shift of our conversations whenever I spoke about my
peace.

It wasn't about my relationship status.
It was about my **freedom**.

I wasn't chasing love to feel complete.
I wasn't desperate for validation.
And that unsettled her.

Because some people can't handle watching you enjoy a season they're struggling to survive.

Some friendships don't break over betrayal.
They break over comparison.

The Friend Who Mocked My Leap

I told another friend I was moving to Las Vegas.
She laughed.
Then said plainly,
"That's stupid."

No concern.
No curiosity.
No support.

What she couldn't see—
what she *wouldn't* see—
was that I wasn't running from something.
I was running **toward myself**.

Las Vegas wasn't an escape.
It was alignment.

That move changed my entire life.
It expanded me.
Healed me.
Introduced me to versions of myself
I never would have met if I had stayed small
to make others comfortable.

Her reaction wasn't about the city.
It was about fear—
fear of change,
fear of risk,
fear of watching me choose a life
she didn't have the courage to imagine.

Some people only support your growth
when it fits inside their understanding.
When it doesn't,
they call it foolish.

I packed my life anyway.
And I was right.

When Trust Breaks

I once trusted a friend with my deepest wounds—
stories I had never spoken aloud.

I believed she would hold them gently,
like fragile glass.

Instead, she passed them around carelessly.
My pain became conversation.
My trauma became commentary.

She promised she wouldn't say a word.
Looked me in the eye and gave me her word.

And then she broke it.

The irony?
We're still cool today.
We laugh, we talk, we share space—
but the trust is gone.
Completely gone.

I had always defended her.
Stood up for her.
Believed in her goodness.

Yet when it mattered most,
she didn't stand up for me.

And I didn't even hear it from her.
One of her brother's girlfriends pulled me aside and said:

"Don't trust her. She's telling all of your personal business."

That sentence stayed with me.

It wasn't just the betrayal—
it was realizing my secrets were floating in rooms
I was never invited into.

That moment taught me this:

Not everyone who listens cares.
Not everyone who promises keeps their word.
Some people love the sound of your secrets
more than the weight of your trust.

Now I smile—
but it's different.
I laugh—
but it's guarded.

Trust is not given.
It's earned.
And once broken,
it rarely returns the same.

When Family Doubts You

I once heard that a family member wished I would fail—
fail in life,
fail in my dreams,
fail in everything I worked for.

When I confronted her,
the discomfort never left.

Because even if she didn't say it,
something was said.

Too many people told me she and her siblings
spoke negatively about me and my ex-husband.
They said I wouldn't succeed when I moved to Vegas.
That I would fall flat.

And yet—
here I am.

Not holding grudges.
Holding boundaries.

I don't trust them.
I can't.
Trust lost to betrayal isn't freely given again.

I'm not perfect.
I have flaws.
I make mistakes.

But I am loyal.
I defend the people I love.
I stand up for them
even when others tear them down.

And maybe that's why the betrayal hurt so deeply—
because I gave what I never received.

Blood doesn't guarantee loyalty.
Family can love you and still doubt you.

When Cousins Cross Lines

One of my closest cousins became close with my husband's
ex-wife—
and I know she did it to hurt me.

What she didn't know
was that people spoke negatively about her—
and I was the one defending her.

She's also the one who told me:

"People don't like being around you."

I'm grateful she said it.
Because I blossomed after that.

Nothing but God.
He knows how to take the trash out.

And I finally understood:

How do you get close to people who don't like me?
Because you don't like me either.

My mother warned me not to be around them.
I didn't listen then—
but I understand now.

When Their Words Became Weapons

There was a time when my family talked more about my marriage
than I did.
Every gathering, every phone call, every little circle of conversation
somehow circled back to my ex-husband cheating.

And the worst part?
I wasn't even around.

I heard it all **from other people**—
people who pulled me aside and said,
"Girl, you should hear how bad they talk about you and your
marriage."

They didn't speak with concern.
They spoke with entertainment.
My pain had become their topic of the day.

"They said he's out here embarrassing you."
"They said he's cheating left and right."
"They said you're stupid for staying."
"They said you must not know what's going on."

Every word was a dagger,
not because it was new information,
but because it came from people who were supposed to love me.

And the whole time, I kept thinking:

**"The tongue is powerful.
Be careful what you speak over someone's life."**

Because while they were busy repeating his sins,
they didn't realize they were planting seeds—
seeds of doubt,
seeds of fear,
seeds of insecurity.

Words can shape a woman's spirit
just as quickly as they can break it.

And the irony?
Some of the same people who talked the loudest
smiled in his face
when they saw him.

They didn't care about my healing.
They cared about the story.

But here's the part they didn't expect:

Every negative word they spoke
became a mirror for me.

A reflection.
A reminder.

Not of his betrayal—
but of theirs.

Because the tongue is powerful.
And when you speak destruction over someone else's life,
you reveal the destruction living inside your own.

Their words didn't break me.
They woke me up.

They taught me that not every voice deserves access to my spirit.
Not every opinion deserves space in my mind.
Not every relative deserves a front-row seat to my life.

Some people talk about your pain
because they're afraid to face their own.

And once I understood that,
I stopped letting their tongues shape my destiny.

I chose silence.
I chose distance.
I chose peace.

And I've been protected ever since.

And Still, I Rise

Smile in your face and speak against you.

And that's okay.

Because **I define me.**
I write my story.
And every step forward proves their predictions wrong.

CHAPTER 10

MY SON, MY HERO

I was twenty-one years old when my life changed forever. At that age, I was focused on my career, chasing dreams, and building a future I thought I had all figured out. Motherhood wasn't part of the plan—not yet. But life has a way of surprising us, and the moment I held my son in my arms, everything shifted. He was perfect. From the very beginning, he was surrounded by love—and yes, spoiled rotten. Both sides of the family adored him. He had everything a child could want, but what mattered most was that he had a good heart. Even as a little boy, he was respectful, kind, and full of life.

And when I looked at him, I saw myself. He was my mirror—my reflection in a smaller frame. People would say, "He looks just like you," and they were right. But it wasn't just his face; it was his spirit. His intelligence, his curiosity, his drive. There was something presidential about the way he carried himself even as a child—calm, observant, wise beyond his years. I used to look at him and think, **This man could be the President of the United States one day.** And I meant it. Not because of titles or power, but because he had the heart, the discipline, the leadership, and the kind of quiet strength that makes people follow him without him ever trying.

As he grew, I watched him blossom into a young man with potential written all over him. But when he turned thirteen, I faced one of the hardest decisions of my life. He had started hanging around the wrong crowd—kids who didn't share his values, kids who could lead him down a dangerous path. I knew I had to act. So, I made a decision that broke my heart but saved his future: I sent him to live with his father.

Not long after, I got a call that shook me. My son and a group of boys had been taken to the precinct. My heart raced as I drove there, praying he hadn't done anything wrong. When I arrived, the officer looked at me and said words I'll never forget: **"Ma'am, your son didn't do anything. He was just with the wrong crowd. But let** me tell you something—your son is a leader, not a follower." I stood there stunned as he continued, **"You raised a very respectful young man. He said 'Yes, sir' and 'No, sir.' That matters— especially because he's a young Black man with manners. The other kids were rude and disrespectful. But your son? He stood out."**

Those words filled me with pride and relief. As we walked out of that precinct, I thought, *I'm doing something right.*

After that, I moved him to Las Vegas to live with his father. He was upset—angry even—but deep down, I knew it was the best decision for his life. I refused to let my son become another statistic, caught in the traps society sets for young Black men. In Vegas, he thrived. His father spoiled him, but I had already laid the foundation: clean the house, take care of his sister, and never depend on a woman for anything.

Three years later, life threw another curveball at us. He was seventeen, a senior in high school, and a star basketball and football athlete, one of the best in Las Vegas. Then one day, he said the words that made my heart drop: **"Mom... I got a girl pregnant."** I cried. Not out of anger, but out of fear. I had dreams for him, and I worried this would change everything. But then I remembered— everything happens for a reason. And that reason came in the form of my grandson. That little boy changed my life for the better.

My son didn't just travel the world—he lived it. Spain. Poland. Oregon. California. Hawaii. Every place became a chapter in his story. He learned new cultures, built new lives, and grew into the man I always knew he could be. He's the kind of man who will drive from Portland to Florida in a heartbeat if his mom needs him. No hesitation. No questions. Just action. That's who he is. Always helping. Always showing up. Always protecting.

And he's sharp—so sharp it amazes me. I can teach him something once, and within seconds, he knows how to do it like he's been doing it his whole life. That kind of intelligence and adaptability makes him unstoppable. I love this guy. Not just because he's my son, but because of the man he has become—the father, the brother, the protector, the heart of our family.

People even walk up to us sometimes and think he's my man because I look so youthful—I must say! I just smile and say, "No, he's, my son." Then we walk away laughing, sharing that private joke only we understood.

Today, he has two sons of his own. They adore their dad. His oldest—now almost sixteen—grew up right alongside him. Their bond is unbreakable. His youngest son... we haven't seen him since he was five. He's ten now. One day, I believe God will open the doors for us to see him again. That part of the story belongs to my son, so I won't elaborate—but I hold on to hope and faith that the reunion will come.

When I look back at my life, I realize every sacrifice, every hard decision, and every tear was worth it. I raised a son who became a man of strength, character, and love—a man who now pours those same values into his own children. Watching him as a father reminds me of the lessons I taught him: respect, responsibility, resilience. He didn't just learn them, **he lives them.**

And there's something I want to say to him, something only a mother can say with her whole heart

Son, I'm sorry for the bad choices I made along the way. I'm sorry for the moments I didn't get right, the decisions that hurt you, and the times life forced you to grow up faster than you should have. But Mom has no regrets—because even through my mistakes, you lived a great life because of them. Everything I did, I did try to protect you, guide you, and give you a bigger future than anything I ever had.

Our journeys are connected. My story as a mother became the foundation for his story as a father. And now, through his sons, the legacy continues. One day, when his children look at him with pride, they will see what I see:

a hero.

My son is my heart, my everything—
and now, he is someone else's hero too.

CHAPTER 11
ALMOST LOSING MY DAUGHTER

I had already buried my mother.
I had already watched my daughter lose her baby boy.
But nothing prepared me for the moment I almost lost *her* too.

Before the emergency, she had been fighting silently for weeks —
swelling, headaches, exhaustion, stress, grief.
But she kept going anyway.

Turning in assignments.
Attending classes.
Pushing through pain she never should've had to endure.

I'll never forget the night she was so swollen she could barely see,
yet she sat there finishing a college paper due that night.
Her laptop rested on her belly while her body was failing her.

I whispered to myself,
"That's my shero."
Not because she was fearless —
but because she refused to quit.

The Call That Changed Everything

We were celebrating when my phone rang.
Her voice trembled through the speaker:

**"Mom… my head… it hurts so bad. I can't see.
My hands and feet are swelling.
Mom, I'm scared."**

Then she said the words that froze every part of me:

"Mom… I don't feel my baby moving."

I ran.
Didn't explain anything to anyone.
Just ran.

When I reached her, she was pale, shaking, swollen, terrified.
I held her and said,

**"I got you.
We're going to the hospital right now."**

I drove like angels cleared the highway.

The Hospital — A Race Against Time

Everything happened fast.

Machines.
Nurses rushing.
Doctors whispering.
Alarms.
Urgency tightening the room.

And in the middle of all that chaos,
a rage started building inside me —
a mother's rage.

Because my daughter had **preeclampsia,**
and the hospital that handled her prenatal care
never monitored her the way they should have.

They missed the signs.
They dismissed her symptoms.
They let her walk around swollen, in pain, barely able to see —
and they didn't take it seriously.

I trusted them with my child.
And they failed her.

That anger still sits in my chest like a stone.

A nurse performed a sonogram.
We heard a heartbeat.
I exhaled —
until she said:

**"That's not the baby.
That's your daughter's heartbeat."**

The doctor came in, looked at the screen,
looked at us, and we already knew.

"I'm so sorry… there is no baby heartbeat."

My daughter screamed a scream no mother ever forgets.
I held her as her world shattered.

Then the doctor said:

"We have to deliver now. Your daughter is very sick."

And all I could do was pray:

"Lord… please don't take my daughter too."

Delivery — Lil Lesiahs Williams

She delivered the sweetest baby boy —
Lil Lesiahs Williams.

Tiny.
Perfect.
Peaceful.

He looked like he was simply resting,
as if he might open his eyes at any moment
and change our world forever.

We held him.
Kissed him.
Took pictures.
Whispered our love into his tiny ears.
Tried to memorize every detail
because we knew our time with him would be measured in moments,
not days.

He was here.
He was beautiful.
He was ours.

Even if only for a moment.

We had him cremated —
a mother and daughter carrying ashes instead of a baby,
a grief too heavy for words.

Even now, the memory slices through me.
But I do not question God.
I trust Him, even when it hurts.

The Moment That Broke Me

After they took the baby, a doctor pulled me aside.
His face told me everything before he even spoke.

**"If we hadn't delivered when we did...
we could have lost her."**

I had just lost my mother.
I had just lost my grandson.
And now I was being told I might lose my daughter too.

Something inside me cracked —
a quiet, devastating break.

But God carried me.
And somehow, my strength carried her.

Healing Together — Rising From Loss

We prayed together.
Cried together.
Held each other through nights that felt endless.
Grief sat between us like a third presence —
heavy, silent, suffocating —
but we faced it side by side.

There were days she couldn't get out of bed.
Days she stared into nothing.
Days she asked God "why" with tears streaming down her face.
And I held her, even when I was breaking too.

But slowly — painfully — she rose.

She Has My Strength — Always Did

Everything she survived —
from her premature birth
to the loss of her own child
to the moment she almost lost her life —
proved she carries my strength.

She inherited my fight.
My endurance.
My spirit.

Three generations of women —
my mother,

me,
my daughter —
all built from God's strongest material.

Five Months Later — Her Triumph

Five months after losing her baby boy…
five months after nearly losing her life…
my daughter walked across the stage at her HBCU
and graduated with Honor Society distinction.

I watched her walk,
head high,
eyes forward,
moving with a strength that made my heart ache.

She didn't just graduate.
She overcame.
She rose.
She conquered.

Her cap and gown weren't just fabric —
they were armor.
Proof that she survived what should have destroyed her.

The Woman She Became

After graduation, she moved away —
built a good career,
found her footing,
and started living her life like it's golden.

Watching her shine brings me joy and pain at the same time.
Because I love her so much
that when I'm hard on her,
it hurts me too.

But I know she is the woman she is today
because I pushed her,
protected her,
and loved her with everything in me.

She is my miracle.
My pride.
My proof that God still writes beauty after tragedy.

And when I look at her now —
alive, strong, thriving —
I know this truth:

**Sometimes the miracle
is simply that she's still here.**

FINAL CHAPTER

LOSING MY ROSE (MOTHER) 91 YEARS OLD

My mother was a smart, wise, caring woman—sharp in her mind, soft in her heart, and steady in her spirit. She carried a quiet intelligence that didn't need to be announced. She understood life deeply, read people effortlessly, and always seemed to know what to say before I even finished speaking. Her wisdom wasn't loud; it was lived. And her love wasn't fragile; it was firm, protective, and intentional.

She was **good with money**, too.
Not cheap. Not stingy.
Smart. Strategic.
She knew how to save, how to plan, how to stretch a dollar with dignity.
But even with all that wisdom, she shared when people needed help.
If someone was struggling, she didn't hesitate.
Her generosity was quiet but constant.

And she loved **quality**.
Even when it came to paper plates, they had to be a certain brand, a certain thickness, a certain standard. She wasn't having anything flimsy in her house.
That was her—classy in the smallest details.

We never wore cheap clothes or cheap shoes.
Not once.
She made sure we looked good, felt good, and carried ourselves with dignity. She put us in private school because she believed in education, in exposure, in excellence. She wanted us to have the best—not to impress anyone, but because she believed we deserved it.

And she could **cook**.
Lord, could she cook.
A great cook in a way that can't even be explained—seasoning with

instinct, feeding people with love, turning simple meals into memories. Her food tasted like comfort, like home, like wisdom passed down through generations.

And through it all, she was **so darn smart**.
A natural brilliance.
A woman whose intuition was sharper than most people's logic.
And the most beautiful part?
She was still that sharp, still that wise, still that brilliant at **91 years old**.
Age never dimmed her mind.
If anything, it made her wisdom richer.

She spoke well—clear, articulate, polished.
Her words carried weight, grace, and intention.
She didn't just talk; she communicated.
And I know that's where I get it from.
My voice, my articulation, my ability to speak with strength and softness at the same time—
that's her in me.

She loved **all her children** until the very day she died.
Every single one.
No favorites.
No conditions.
Just pure, steady, unwavering love.

And with me?
She never told me no.
Not because she spoiled me, but because she trusted me.
She believed in who I was becoming long before I fully did.

Before I became her caregiver...
Before I held her as she transitioned...
Before hospitals, medications, and final goodbyes—

She was my girl.
My everything.
My safe place.

My soft landing.
My favorite human in the world.

And I miss her so much that sometimes I get physically sick thinking about living without her.
The kind of missing that hits in the stomach, not the mind.
The kind that makes breathing feel heavy.
The kind that reminds you that love this deep never dies—it just changes form.

Everything Changed in a Moment

My mother died in front of me.

Writing that still shakes something loose inside my spirit—something that will never fully settle again.

And what makes it even harder is what happened **the day before**.

My nephew had come to Florida to visit her.
He walked into the room, took one look at her, and said,
"Auntie... she's not going to be here long."

I looked at him like he had lost his mind.
I said,
"Boy, please. That woman will be here forever."

Because in my eyes, she was unshakeable.
She was strong.
She was wise.
She was still sharp at 91.
She was *my mother.*
Forever felt like the only option.

But the next day...
she died.

He was right.
And I wasn't ready.

And the hardest part wasn't just losing her—
it was having to call my siblings and tell them she was gone.
My voice broke.
My heart broke.
Because I know she was 91. .
but that was **my mommy**.

And the truth is this:
all the marriages I lost, all the heartbreak I survived, all the endings I walked through—none of it amounts to losing my girl.
Nothing compares.
Nothing even comes close.

She had just come home from the hospital.
She was smiling.
Talking.
Looking at my daughter with tenderness in her eyes.

We thought we had time.
We truly believed she was recovering.

My son and grandson had just arrived to help care for her.
We were preparing for healing.
Not goodbye.

But grief doesn't wait for preparation.

One moment she was here.
The next moment—she wasn't.

I held her hand.
Called her name.
Tried to hold onto her spirit as it slipped away.

Part of me wishes I could erase that moment forever.
Another part is grateful I was there—
that her last voice was mine,
that she didn't leave this world alone.

When Grief Turned to Fear

There was a moment no one saw.
A moment when the grief didn't come out as tears, but as rage.

I hit the wall.
Not because I was violent,
but because my body needed somewhere to put the pain.

My hands shook.
My chest burned.
My heart raced like it was trying to outrun reality.

I was so overwhelmed by anger and fear that I became afraid to close
my eyes.
Afraid that if I did, I wouldn't be able to breathe.
Afraid that if I let go even for a second, I would completely fall apart.
Afraid that sleep would mean surrender—and I didn't feel safe
surrendering.

My body was in survival mode.
My nervous system was screaming.
My spirit didn't know where to land.

I wasn't angry at her.
I was angry at the suddenness.
At the unfairness.
At the way life stole her without warning.

That was the moment grief stopped being something I felt
and became something that lived inside my body.

And after she died, I gained weight—
not because I was eating,
but because I slipped into a depression I didn't even recognize.
My body was grieving even when my mind was numb.
I didn't know I was depressed.
I just knew I was hurting in ways I couldn't explain.

The Love That Remains

My mother didn't just leave this world — she **left a legacy**.
A legacy of wisdom, class, generosity, and quiet strength that still
lives in me.

She was the kind of woman whose presence filled a room without
raising her voice.
The kind of woman who stayed sharp, witty, and wise all the way to
91.
The kind of woman who taught through example, not speeches.

She left me full—
of her wisdom,
her strength,
her class,
her courage,
her voice,
her love.

Her absence broke me open
Her memory is putting me back together,
piece by piece,
as a stronger, softer, more honest woman.

Grief is not the enemy of healing.
It is the doorway to it.

And even now—
I don't remember everything from that time—
but I remember her.

And that has been enough to keep me alive.

FINAL CHAPTER

I AM FREE, I AM WHOLE

Becoming the woman I needed wasn't a moment.
It wasn't a breakthrough, a revelation, or a single day where
everything suddenly made sense.
It was a becoming — slow, intentional, and earned.

It happened in the quiet places,
in the nights I cried myself empty,
in the mornings I chose to rise anyway,
in the decisions no one saw but changed everything.

It happened when I stopped abandoning myself.
When I stopped shrinking to make others comfortable.
When I stopped confusing endurance with love.
When I stopped calling survival "strength."

Becoming the woman I needed meant returning to myself —
to the girl who once believed she could do anything,
to the woman who learned she could survive anything,
and to the future version of me who refused to settle for anything
less than peace.

It meant honoring my intuition,
trusting my voice,
and choosing myself even when it disappointed others.

It meant letting go of the woman I pretended to be
so I could finally embrace the woman I truly am.

There was a time when I didn't know what I wanted.
I only knew what I had survived.
I knew what I had lost.
I knew how to show up for everyone else —
how to perform strength,

how to keep moving when everything in me
was begging for rest.

But I didn't know *me*.
Not beyond the roles I wore like armor:
Mother.
Wife.
Sister.
Friend.
Fixer.

For so long, my identity was shaped by who I was to everyone else
—
their needs,
their comfort,
their expectations.
I became fluent in sacrifice,
fluent in endurance,
fluent in disappearing.

Somewhere along the way,
I stopped asking myself the question
that would change everything:

What do I want?

And when I finally asked it,
the answer wasn't a title,
a relationship,
a reinvention,
or a brand-new life.

It was a feeling.
A truth.
A whisper rising from a place in me
I had ignored for years:

I want to feel safe inside myself.

Safe in my choices.
Safe in my boundaries.
Safe in my voice.
Safe in my own presence.

And with that truth came another:
I have always been smart.
I have always been wise.
But now —
I no longer live to please anyone.
I no longer shrink, bend, or sacrifice myself to keep the peace.
I know how to say *no* when something doesn't serve me,
doesn't honor me,
or doesn't feel right in my spirit.

For the first time in my life,
I allowed myself to want things —
real things,
joyful things,
things that belonged to me.

I want to travel.
I want to make money.
I want to go to the beach and let the sun remind me I survived.
I want to laugh without looking over my shoulder.
I want to rest without guilt.
I want a life that feels like freedom,
not obligation.

And the beautiful part is —
I no longer wait for permission.
I no longer wait for someone to choose me.
I choose myself.
Every day.
In every decision.
In every boundary.
In every dream I allow myself to imagine.

This —
this knowing,

this choosing,
this claiming of myself —
was the beginning of real healing.

Healing wasn't loud.
It wasn't dramatic.
It wasn't a single moment.
It was a returning —
to my voice,
to my intuition,
to the woman I had always been becoming.

I learned that peace is not something you find.
It's something you build.
Brick by brick.
Boundary by boundary.
Truth by truth.

And now, standing in the fullness of who I am,
I know this with certainty:

I walked through fire and came out carrying my own light.
I rebuilt myself piece by piece, truth by truth, boundary by boundary,
until the woman I used to pray for finally rose inside me.
Today, I stand in a life I shaped with my own hands —
a life rooted in peace, clarity, and self-worth.
I am no longer defined by what I endured.
I am defined by what I chose next.
I am free.
I am whole.
And I am finally, beautifully, me.

And when they hold me,
I'll know the difference between a man who took from me
and a man God sent to love me.

I am healed now.
I am whole now.

And I am ready for a love that mirrors the man God is shaping
you to be.

So, when God places us in front of each other,
come with those same hands —
steady, gentle, grown, and godly.

Because I have already survived
what broken hands can do.

I am ready to be loved
by the right ones.

ABOUT THE AUTHOR

I am a college graduate with a bachelor's degree whose life is rooted in resilience, discipline, and purpose. Entrepreneurial since the age of fifteen, I learned early how to create opportunities, navigate uncertainty, and build from vision rather than circumstance.

I trained as a cosmetologist in my younger years, an experience that sharpened my creativity and deepened my connection to people from all walks of life. Through that work, I learned how closely identity, healing, and self-expression are intertwined. Over time, my path expanded, and I became a tax preparer, certified life coach, actress, and author—each role reflecting a commitment to growth, storytelling, and service.

My work is informed by lived experience, not theory. I write from a place of survival, transformation, and hard-earned wisdom. I have lived in New Jersey, Maryland, Las Vegas, and Florida, and each place shaped my understanding of people, relationships, resilience, and reinvention.

As a mother, a survivor, and a woman of faith, I believe healing is both personal and generational. My voice is rooted in truth, accountability, and restoration. This book is not only a reflection of where I've been, but a testament to what is possible when pain is faced, named, and transformed.

I continue to evolve—learning, unlearning, and becoming. My story is still being written.